PRACTICE OF EDUCATION IN TRINIDAD AND TOBAGO –

Does it Infringe on the Human Rights

of Disabled Students?

Libert Education

ISBN 978-0-6151-7133-3

PRACTICE OF EDUCATION IN TRINIDAD AND TOBAGO –

Does it Infringe on the Human Rights of Disabled Students?

Derived from Dissertation submitted in part requirement for the

Master of Education in Special and Inclusive Education of the

University of Sheffield, December 2001

PRINTED IN THE UNITED STATES OF AMERICA

ISBN 978-0-6151-7133-3

PRACTICE OF EDUCATION IN TRINIDAD AND TOBAGO –

Does it Infringe on the Human Rights of Disabled Students?

Rodney A. Libert, T.Dip.(VTC), Dip.Sp.Ed., M.Ed.-SIE(Shef).

Special Education Teacher

Thomas Weaver High School

Hartford, Connecticut USA

ABSTRACT

This investigation sought to determine if the human rights of disabled students are being met in the system of education in Trinidad and Tobago. A survey was conducted to gather information from teachers of special schools in the country.

The study revealed that physical adaptations in special schools are lacking. Teachers are generally not properly trained to provide for children with special education needs, resulting in poor implementation of the curriculum.

It was recommended that government should invest in providing access to all students and teachers should make maximum use of existing teaching aids. Teachers' attitudes towards disabled persons should be changed with the appropriate training and education. In addition, teachers should be trained in matters of curriculum implementation.

ACKNOWLEDGEMENTS

Thanks to Almighty God Who makes all things possible.

Special thanks to my wife and children for their patience throughout this process.

Thanks to all those teachers who participated in the survey for their honest responses and helpful comments.

To my tutors, Dr. Launcelot Brown and Dr. Joan Pedro, for their invaluable contributions and encouragement, I offer special thanks.

Thanks to Professor Derrick Armstrong for his patience and advice. Dr. Ann Cheryl Armstrong, thanks for your advice.

Special thanks to all my friends who continue to encourage and inspire me.

DEFINITION OF TERMS

Afro-Trinbagonian	A citizen of Trinidad and Tobago of predominantly African descent.
Afro-Zimbabwean	A citizen of Zimbabwe of African descent.
Amerindians	The native peoples of the 'New World' originally referred to as American Indians
Arawaks	A peaceful people of Amerindian origin from South Trinidad.
Caribs	A conquering people of Amerindian origin from Central and East Trinidad.
Concordat	A 1960 agreement between denominational school boards and the Government of Trinidad and Tobago to provide Primary and Secondary education.
Euro-Zimbabwean	A citizen of Zimbabwe of European descent.
Indo-Trinbagonian	A citizen of Trinidad and Tobago of Indian descent.
Mixed-Trinbagonian	A citizen of Trinidad and Tobago of mixed ancestry.
Ward Schools	Community schools.

LIMITATIONS

Obtaining information from the Ministry of Education proved to be almost impossible because of a lack of information on Special Education in Trinidad and Tobago. In addition, during my literature search, I found that research on human rights in education was non-existent in my country. I therefore had to shift the focus of my study from the disabled students in mainstream schools to students in special schools.

Although I submitted application for permission to conduct research some four months in advance, my letter could not be traced. With the help of a relative, I received that permission some three years after I had relocated to the United States.

Relocation impacted negatively on my research. I had problems with retrieving all of my literature, especially newspaper and magazine clippings, and was forced to make costly trips in order to gather data. Even with the use of the Internet, information on Special Education in Trinidad and Tobago was impossible to come by. I remained with very little to work with and no support for a very long time. But persistence paid well.

TABLE OF CONTENTS

Chapter 1
Introduction

STATEMENT OF THE PROBLEM

The Government of Trinidad and Tobago (1985) Education Plan states that:

The Government accepts its role as the responsible agency for providing Special Education at all levels of the Education System...in the regular public school (with additional supporting services) e.g. in the main stream or in special classes..." *("Education plan 1985-1990", 1985); p. 63)*

This statement is not in keeping with The Education Policy Paper 1993 to 2003 that states that 80% of children who were assessed by the Child Guidance Clinic and identified with special education needs are receiving inappropriate education. Lloyd Best, in his commentary in the Trinidad Express Newspapers of May 29, 2000, states that even though schools admit anyone from any community, and the curriculum is designed for all, still only a few, the élite, are catered for in the system. If this is indeed so, then there may be questions that the rights of the disabled are being infringed.

Article 23 (1) of the United Nations Convention on the Rights of the Child (1989) states: -

'State Parties recognise that a mentally or physically disabled child should enjoy a full and decent life, in conditions which ensure dignity, promote self-reliance and facilitate the child's active participation in the community.'

In Trinidad and Tobago, we sing in our National Anthem *'...here every creed and race find an equal place....'*. A nine-year-old boy who contracted an ear infection and became profoundly deaf by the time he was ten did not *'find an equal place'*. In spite of his intelligence, his interests, his desires, he was unable to continue his education at his village school and his single parent could not afford to send his son to a school for deaf children, even if there were space at the schools. Without this opportunity for an education, he was left without dignity and dependent on others. He was unable to participate actively in the community, not even in the deaf community.

A young lady who used a wheelchair to get around the secondary school she attended did not *'find an equal place'*. Ramps were crudely constructed to accommodate her on the ground floor but every time she needed to use the lavatory, she depended on her peers to assist her. This reliance on her friends diminished her dignity. In addition, she had no access to the library, which was on the floor above her classroom. This made it impossible for her to actively participate in the school community.

The deaf young lady who was very much interested in further education did not *'find an equal place'*. She enrolled in a certificate course in early childhood education, indicating that she was deaf. She was accepted. Unfortunately, she experienced a lot of difficulty in doing some courses because, in the absence of an interpreter, some lecturers could not, or would not adjust their teaching styles to accommodate her. She said that at these times she was totally dependent on her peers for information and was unable to participate in any class discussions. She felt completely alienated.

Chimedza and Dzvimbo (1995) state that very little provision was made for the education of Afro-Zimbabwean children. The system was examination centred with tests and examinations being used to select persons at each grade level. Few persons were able to obtain secondary placement, resulting in very little chances for children with disabilities to benefit from education.

Trinidad and Tobago had - and still has to some extent - the same examination centred approach with competition to obtain secondary school places, thus effectively eliminating persons with special education needs. In an attempt to provide the best education we can for our children in our competitive and selective examination centred education system, we must, like the Maltese (Bartolo, 1995), send our children to private lessons after school and on weekends to increase their chances of gaining selection for a space in a 'prestige' secondary school. In the process, anxiety and frustration set in for both parents and children, thus creating a greater special education need for these children. Even today, with an expansion of the education system resulting in more secondary school places, children with special education needs are at a great disadvantage.

Lavia (1995) argues that historically, disabled persons have not been catered for in the education system of Trinidad and Tobago. In this study I questioned if the practice of education in Trinidad and Tobago infringes on the human rights of disabled students.

BACKGROUND OF THE PROBLEM

After seventeen years as an educator in Trinidad and Tobago, this researcher entered this research as a Special Educator, an ordinary, concerned citizen of Trinidad and Tobago and as a parent. My children often look to me for explanations for the injustices they see being handed down by society, to persons with disabilities and persons who may be at risk.

Paranjpe (1994) tells us that there is a lack of research, data and published material concerning special education in India. This can be said to be the same in Trinidad and Tobago since special education is new to our country. Trinidad and Tobago, a former British colony, emerged from the colonial system with only a small percentage of the population being educated.

O'Leary (1997) tells us that in Somalia,

'The colonial education policies...had limited objectives, namely, the training of a small number of educated Somalis to fill the limited job opportunities in public administration and ...the demand for trained human resources in the private sector.'
(p. 64).

The idea was to educate just enough persons to run the affairs of the colonial government and have the rest of the population completely dependent on them, the colonial government. This is exactly the present position of disabled and disadvantaged persons in many developing countries today - they are dependent on charity from the government and non-governmental organisations.

Chimedza and Dzvimbo (1995) and Coleridge (1993) state that historically, rural dwellers, who compose the majority of people in Zimbabwe, thought of disability as a show of displeasure by ancestors or a curse associated with punishment for evil deeds and as witchcraft. Congenital conditions, says Coleridge (1993), were viewed as the proof of a mother's infidelity.

As a result, disability was seen as an embarrassment to the families of disabled persons. The culture of the people therefore placed disabled people in a class of their own. Because it was felt that these children were 'doomed' for the rest of their lives, the general feeling was that they did not belong in the regular classes and so special schools were established in 1927 in Zimbabwe to cater for children with visual impairments. Other special schools followed.

In India, the Hindu religious belief in reincarnation is that disability is a punishment for sins committed by the disabled person in a former life (Coleridge, 1993). The disabled person therefore deserves the 'God given' punishment and accepts it because that is his/her *karma* or destiny (ibid.). Parents and the community therefore have negative attitudes towards education of disabled children. The community is not aware of facts regarding disabilities and their associated needs and problems.

More than ninety 90% of the present population, according to the 1990 census (Central Statistical Office, 1994), of Trinidad and Tobago are descendants of native Indians and native Africans who were brought to our shores as indentured labourers or as slaves. Though there have been changes in the cultures of both peoples through socialisation and oppression, they have been able to maintain some aspects of their original cultures, especially the Indo-Trinbagonian, who were not exposed to the forced suppression of their native languages, religions and customs.

We therefore have, in Trinidad and Tobago, adopted some of the beliefs of the Indians and Africans as far as disability is concerned. In addition, the influence of the British, Spanish, French, Caribs and Arawaks, make Trinidad and Tobago's culture a potpourri. Like other countries of the world, the historical perceptions of disabilities have influenced the social and cultural factors, which affect the education of children with special education needs in Trinidad and Tobago. Education of disabled persons began with charitable organisations, religious bodies and individuals who dared to think and be different.

The Education Policy Paper 1993 – 2003 (1993) states that there are two government and eight assisted special schools in Trinidad and Tobago. These assisted special schools were established by Non-Governmental Organisations (NGO's) from 1943 to 1986. The two government-run special schools were established in 1988.

The Education Act of 1966 of Trinidad and Tobago did not mandate provision for children with special education needs. The Act states: -

> *"39. (1) The Minister may: -*
> *(a) cause to be established any special*
> *school..." (p. 24)*

Over the years, government has seconded teachers to these NGO's to provide the necessary education to the children with special needs. A few teachers were sent abroad for specialised training in the 1970's and 1980's.

In 1981, the establishment of a Special Education Unit meant the beginning of the incorporation of Special Schools run by NGO's into the education system. During the decade of the 1980's, a National

Introduction

Survey of Disabled Children in Trinidad and Tobago was carried out by Dr. Michael Marge of Syracuse University on behalf of the Organisation of American States (The Marge Report, 1984). This report identified some 27,000 or 16.1% of children between the ages of three and sixteen with some type of disability (p. 28b). The Ministry of Education combined their efforts with the Canadian International Development Agency (CIDA) and Inter-America Development Bank (IADB) to provide workshops and seminars to assist teachers, principals and supervisors in catering to the needs of our disabled children. The Pilgrim Report of 1990 states that: -

> *'Any attempt to provide adequate and appropriate education for students with learning difficulties...implies the provision of professional studies in special education.'*
> *(Government of Trinidad and Tobago, 1990, p. 47)*

Special Education was introduced as an elective subject at the Valsayn Teachers' College in the late 1980s where a small number of student teachers were exposed to the principles and practice of Special Education. It was introduced to all student teachers as a module in 1994. In preparation for integration, teachers were sent to secondary schools in order to sensitise the staff of the schools to prepare for the integration of disabled children, especially the hearing impaired children. A concession in the form of extra time was given to disabled children writing the Common Entrance Examination. All NGO's involved in the education and care of disabled children are given grants by the Ministry of Education. Resource services are provided by the Guidance Unit, the Curriculum Unit, the Training Unit and the Measurement Unit of the Ministry.

Government has not seen it fit to allocate sufficient resources towards education. Two setbacks for disabled children in schools are lack of equipment and inappropriate infrastructure. Since Trinidad and Tobago has only recently begun providing for our disabled population, our buildings have not been constructed in the past to accommodate wheelchair users, visually impaired persons or any disabled person at all. The equipment used in mainstream schools is also inappropriate at times and additional equipment necessary for students with hearing impairments or visual impairments is not available.

The government's lack of proper distribution of funds to provide sufficient, trained personnel has impacted negatively on schools, especially those in rural areas (Keller et al, 1993). Although some trained personnel are available, lack of funding makes it difficult to have the teachers proportionally distributed and properly compensated.

According to Lavia (1995), special education issues continued to be overshadowed by bureaucratic objectives rather than educational objectives.

THE PURPOSE OF THE STUDY

This study focused on the rights of disabled children in special schools in Trinidad and Tobago. I analysed the responses of the teachers of these special schools in order to determine if the schools are meeting the rights of disabled children. This information is valuable in order to sensitise significant persons on the equal rights of disabled persons and to suggest ways in which the human rights of disabled students can be assured.

My study sought to answer the following research questions:-

(a) Are special schools sufficiently prepared to offer an equal chance to students with special needs?

(b) How do teacher expectations of disabled students in special schools affect the content delivery?

OVERVIEW OF THE CHAPTERS

In Chapter 1, the Statement of the Problem, the Background of the Problem and the Purpose of the Study provided the foundation for the development of this study. The topic was introduced with the research questions to be answered and relevant definitions were stated.

The following chapter, Chapter 2 is the Review of the Literature. In this chapter I sought to present the place of Special Education in the System of Education in Trinidad and Tobago. Some of the major international Human Rights policies and their relevance to Special Education Services in Trinidad and Tobago were discussed. Experiences of Special Needs Individuals were also shared.

In Chapter 3 I outlined the methodology used to capture and collate data for this presentation.

In Chapter 4, the data were interpreted and the findings discussed.

Chapter 5 contains conclusion, recommendations and general observations, which could serve as a guide for future projects.

Chapter 2

Literature Review

EDUCATION IN TRINIDAD & TOBAGO

In this chapter, I present a brief history of Trinidad and Tobago and its education system to illustrate the place of Special Education within the Education System of this country. I then explore the major Human Rights issues that underpin this research.

A BRIEF HISTORY OF TRINIDAD AND TOBAGO

Trinidad and Tobago, commonly referred to as a twin island republic, are the most southerly isles of the Caribbean, situated just six (6) miles or ten (10) kilometres off the eastern coast of Venezuela in South America. The islands were claimed by Columbus, for Spain, in the fifteenth century. Trinidad was surrendered to the British in 1797 and the islands continued to have separate histories until 1889, when they were united under one British Governor.

In order to boost the failing sugarcane production and for other tasks, African slaves were brought to Trinidad and the other colonies in the seventeenth century (17C). In 1834, after emancipation, ex-slaves, who were offered jobs on plantations, refused to return to such gruelling work and so the authorities looked elsewhere for its labour force. Indians, and to a lesser extent, Chinese, were brought to Trinidad as indentured labourers in the mid nineteenth century (19C), the first indentured labourers arriving from India in 1845. Because of the vast differences in language, religion and culture, the Indians did not socialise with other ethnic groups of the population during their early days here. However, because of the need for upward social movement in society, some of them socialised and even changed their lifestyles to be accommodated in the mainstream of society. They were not forced, like the African slaves before them, to abandon their religions and customs. Unlike the Africans who were separated from their other family members, the Indians and Chinese lived with their families and so were able to practice their family life, languages, customs and religions (Williams, 1962 and 1970).

Trinidad and Tobago gained independence from Britain in 1962 and became a Republic in 1976. The population of 1,213,700 (1990 census) consists of 39.6% Afro-Trinbagonians, 40.3% Indo-Trinbagonians, 18.4% of Mixed-Trinbagonians and 1.6% other ethnic descendants. The majority of the population is Christian, 23.2% are Hindus and 5.8% are Muslims.

THE HISTORY OF EDUCATION IN TRINIDAD & TOBAGO

1797 – 1850

In 1797, when the British captured Trinidad from the Spaniards, the population then was mainly French settlers, running from war in the other islands, bringing with them, their slaves who were freed. People came into the society from different places at different times for different reasons. As a result, there was a French cultural dominance with Spanish laws and a large number of 'free coloured' persons. The problem the British had then was how to make this place a British region with the French being Roman Catholic. The idea then was to Anglicise, control and civilise the people through the use of education (Keller, 1993). In 1817, all schools were required to be registered (Independence Exhibition Committee, 1962). This is the first record of state involvement in education. Before 1834 when slavery was abolished, private teachers taught children of the 'Free Classes' only (ibid.). Between 1835 and 1842, the British Government allocated an annual sum of 20,000 pounds sterling for the construction of school buildings in its former slave colonies in South Africa and the West Indies. Some of these funds were used to build schools throughout Trinidad for the children of freed slaves (ibid.). Several religious bodies, with the help of state funds, established schools to keep their religious education alive on the colony. They were required to teach religion and they taught all subjects from religious texts. In 1846, the Governor Lord Harris established Ward Schools and stated that wherever these Government schools were built, religious denominations were not allowed to build schools (Keller, 1993).

By the mid 1800's, religious bodies controlled education with grants from the government (ibid.). The influx of East Indians added religious and communication problems to the education system because the new arrivals did not speak English and they were non-Christians.

1851 - 1900

The year 1851 saw the first education policy. Local authorities were given the responsibilities of constructing secular schools and providing education for all children in their districts. These local authorities were governed by a Board of Education led by the Governor and comprising laymen. English was the medium of instruction and the compulsory language at these schools. Wherever these schools were built, aid to denominational schools was stopped (Missen et al, 1954; I.E.C., 1962). Still, they continued and even expanded with the addition of the Presbyterian Church of Canada in 1868 (I.E.C., 1962). These Canadian Missions brought their religion to the East Indians and any other groups in the Territory who were being neglected (Keller, 1993).

In 1852, two teachers' colleges were built in Port of Spain (I.E.C., 1962). The Roman Catholic Church established the St. Mary's College for boys and the St. Joseph Convent for ladies of class in 1856. Missionary Schools taught all areas other than just the basics and payment to teachers was based on results. At that time, the primary purpose of the State Education System was to provide the people with an education that would ensure the basic skills for life. The teachers were well trained but were frustrated because they were told to teach only these basic elements. Parents, who believed that their children should learn something more than just the basics, resisted by keeping their children away from school. This led to the establishing of laws making it illegal for a child to be out of school. These laws for compulsory schooling came about before the system could accommodate all the children (Keller, 1993).

In 1859, the first government boys' secondary school, Queen's Collegiate, was started in Port of Spain (Missen et al, 1954; I.E.C., 1962). The students of Queen's Collegiate School were the first colony pupils to be eligible to sit the Cambridge Examinations and all schools had to be affiliated to the Queen's Collegiate Schools to enable their students to do these examinations (I.E.C., 1962).

Because of the failure of the ward schools, an enquiry into the state of education was launched in 1869. This investigation was conducted by Lord Keenan, who noted that denominational schools were doing better. He recommended a dual relationship where the state would subsidise the denominational schools, or all schools should be handed over to the various denominations, and monitors should be used as teachers (I.E.C., 1962 and Keller, 1993).

The Education Ordinance of 1870 began dual control in education where government schools were fully supported by public funds and denominational schools were assisted through financial aid from the government (Missen et al, 1954; I.E.C., 1962; Keller, 1993). This Ordinance also established three (3) scholarships from primary to secondary schools and four from secondary schools to U.K. Universities (Missen et al, 1945). By 1872, boys who did well in the College Exhibition Examination were being admitted to the Queen's Royal College, formally the Queen's Collegiate School and in 1884, the Presbyterian Church established a boys' secondary school in San Fernando (Keller, 1993).

In 1899, when Tobago became a ward of Trinidad, Tobago's population consisted of freed slaves and some 'coloured' people whose children attended 28 denominational schools. When these schools were combined with the government and denominational schools of Trinidad, the colony had at the turn of the century: -

- 56 government primary schools with 6,973 students on roll and an expenditure of $49,545.60,

- 183 assisted primary schools with 23,146 students on roll and an expenditure of $113,222.40,

- one government secondary school with 100 boys on roll and

- two assisted secondary schools with 250 boys on roll.

The total secondary school expenditure was $1,291.20 and 5,846 primary school places were unused (I.E.C., 1962). Missen et al (1954) states that there were 150 assisted schools in 1902. This possibly excluded the Tobago schools, which became part of the system three (3) years earlier.

1901 - 1925

During the first quarter of the twentieth century (20th C), Trinidad and Tobago was under direct colonial rule. Very little changes took place in the education system, but those changes were very significant. In 1901-1902, the government decided to pay the entire salaries of teachers of the assisted schools. In 1912, these same teachers were afforded the privilege of pension just like their counterparts in government schools (Missen et al, 1954; I.E.C., 1962.).

The year 1914 saw the birth of the Association in Aid of the Blind (M.Ed. Students, 1993), a largely volunteer charity group.

1920 brought on the Era of Nationalism. Recession hit the world. Political thinking changed after the war and people's rights were being championed. There was a growth in democracy and people started to pay more attention to psychology and psychological thinking (Keller, 1993). In 1921, because of mounting pressure from the expanding middle class, five intermediate schools were established to cater for the growing number of students who were caught between the exclusive secondary schools and the ordinary primary schools. Two of these schools were government and three were Roman Catholic schools. A Central Training College for Trinidad was discussed in 1921 and that same year, the Compulsory Education Ordinance was passed with the Governor proclaiming Port of Spain and St. James as compulsory areas (I.E.C., 1962). Missen et al, (1954) states that Port of Spain and St. James became compulsory areas in 1935.

By 1923, systematic inspection of schools replaced the rigid examination of pupils as a means to determine a school's quality and in 1925, Boards of Managers were appointed to replace individuals who controlled appointments, transfers and dismissals of teachers (I.E.C., 1962.).

1926 - 1951

Books were published especially for West Indian children in 1928 by the Senior Inspector of Schools in Trinidad and Tobago, Capt. J. O. Cutteridge (I.E.C., 1962). By 1930, Cutteridge, Mariott and Mayhew, all Caucasian Englishmen, were Directors of Education in Trinidad and Tobago. They were opposed when they tried to introduce psychology in education. A large number of the 'coloured' population were now professionals, contributing vocally to society (Keller, 1993).

1932 saw teachers dissatisfied with the Teachers' Union of Trinidad and Tobago. Headmasters broke away and formed the Teachers' Economic and Cultural Association (TECA). This came about because of two main reasons: -

1) There was a larger number of local teachers, and

2) Black people were now in a number of professional areas and being well paid, therefore the status of the teacher appeared to have dropped.

As TECA started to emphasise people's awareness, the People's Education Movement (PEM) was formed (Keller, 1993).

The 1935 Regulations for Primary Schools abolished the uniform curriculum, requiring teachers to formulate schemes of work more suited to the community in which they taught. Teaching methods and techniques became more practical and visual aids were introduced. Integration of subjects was attempted with less emphasis on grammar. Domestic Science and Woodwork were taught at approved Centres and grants to assisted schools were increased to afford apparatus and equipment. The Private School Ordinance of 1936 gave government

> '...the right of supervision and control of buildings, classrooms, furniture, sanitary arrangements and the general health of the pupils.' (I.E.C., 1962; p.4.)

In 1939, World War II began but there was an overall improvement in infrastructure and provisions for pupils by 1940. Students enjoyed free transport to and from school and there was a daily distribution of milk and meals in Port of Spain and San Fernando geared towards children of less fortunate socio-economic background (ibid.). Missen et al, 1954 states that the free distribution of milk in Port of Spain was inaugurated in 1948 with the meals being included some time after through voluntary organisations. By 1954, 10% of the children attending school benefited from this distribution.

The year 1943 saw the establishment of a Charter for the Association in Aid of the Blind and the formation of the Association in Aid of the Deaf and Dumb (M.Ed. Students, 1993). From 1944 all children from six to twelve years old, living within two miles of a school were required by law to attend school. However, no information was available as to whether or not the children were actually attending. Records of the Registrar General showed that by the 1954 – 1955 school year, an increase of 10 000 school places was necessary to cater for the growing population. In an attempt at accounting for what they described as *'lost children'*, Missen et al, (1954) stated

> *'Some Blind, Deaf and Physically Handicapped children attend schools not under the control of the Education Department; but some do not get any schooling.' (p. 25)*

Missen et al suggest that the shift arrangement should be *'...entirely condemned on educational grounds' (p. 26)*. They stated that *'...only a dire necessity could justify such action.' (ibid)*

No recommendations were made to cater for children who needed Special Education services.

Towards the end of the war, persons moved away from agriculture into employment in the U.S. Military Base. Then came the downfall of the economy. Very high premium was placed on Education since the right to education was set out in the United

Nations Charter. Development was important and the country had to find a way to attract capital. Laws were therefore passed to allow any foreign investors to do industrial business in Trinidad and Tobago without being taxed. The goal was to attract money and to develop the education system. Unfortunately, crises were created because employment was not generated as expected and people saw the situation as one group exploiting another (Keller, 1993).

The Development Program Council Paper No. 27 of 1946 recommended free education for children five to twelve years old at Primary Schools and Building of Central Schools for twelve to fifteen year olds who did not enter Secondary Schools. This group had been a concern and to facilitate evaluation of their education, the School Leaving Certificate was introduced in 1948. Selected graduates of this examination were given places in secondary schools, with the hope of further training as teachers (I.E.C., 1962). Unfortunately, this council paper was never debated, though more than 22,000 primary school places were provided and three secondary schools built and funds made available for full sanitary installations and the cost of the assisted schools. Still, no school was built to cater for the twelve to fifteen year age group who did not enter secondary school and a number of other issues were left undone (Missen et al, 1954).

1946 also saw the establishment of the Cascade School for the Deaf by the Association in Aid of the Deaf and Dumb. 1950 saw the beginning of the National Association for Retarded Children and in 1951, the School for the Blind began operating (M.Ed. Students, 1993). El Socorro Islamic School was the first non-Christian denominational school to be recognised by the government in 1951 (I.E.C., 1962).

Exactly 100 years after Lord Harris introduced the first education policy document, there were: -

- 304 primary schools and 8 intermediate schools with 120,847 students on roll or 85% of the estimated school population
- nine Handicraft Centres serving 90 schools and seven sub-centres at primary schools
- eighteen Domestic Science Centres serving 88 schools and twelve sub-centres at primary schools
- thirteen secondary schools with 6,074 students on roll and sixteen registered private secondary schools with 3,827 on roll. (I.E.C., 1962)

1952 – 1962

During the 1950's, the Association for the Physically Handicapped opened its doors, establishing the Princess Elizabeth Home for the Physically Handicapped and its school in 1953. In 1958, the School for the Mentally Handicapped joined the growing number of special schools (M.Ed. Students, 1993). Since 1906, industries took full responsibility for technical education with grants from the state, but in 1954, the first government Technical School was established in San Fernando. This same year a survey of the education system was done by three foreign educators. This Missen Working Party

> *'…re-emphasised the problems of an unrealistic curriculum and obsolete methods. It severely criticised the College Examination as a means of entrance to a secondary school.'* *(I.E.C., 1962; p. 5)*

Using the monitor system, before 1955, students qualified through the pupil teacher system to be awarded the Teachers' Certificate. From 1955, this certificate was only to be awarded to teachers who graduated from a recognised Teachers' Training College. In addition, the School Teachers' Pension Ordinance of 1955 included for the first time,

> '...teachers in Training Colleges, Industrial Schools, Orphanages, Institute for the Blind, and made provisions for increased gratuity for the dependants of a deceased teacher.'
> (IEC, 1962; p.4)

The Code of Regulations of 1955 brought teachers and civil servants under the same regulations, which restricted their involvement in politics and writing to the press.

Another committee, the Hammond Committee, in 1956, recommended

> '...a fairer system of grants to assisted secondary schools and the same salaries and pension rights for teachers in assisted secondary schools as those in government schools.' (I.E.C., 1962; p. 4)

Government accepted the recommendation. However, in the opinion of the People's National Movement (PNM), formally the PEM, the state was not playing an important enough part in the education system (Keller, 1993).

In 1957, a Regional Conference on Teacher Training suggested an accelerated program. That same year, the Maurice Education Committee began to re-examine the educational needs and problems of Trinidad and Tobago. The committee comprised individuals from various communities around the territory, contributing different views (I.E.C., 1962). The Committee's recommendations in 1959 resulted in more primary schools being built to cater for the five to eleven year age group.

Still, more schools were needed to accommodate the growing number of school-aged children. The Concordat of 1960, an agreement between the denominational school boards and the government was signed, merging government authority and denominational rights and responsibilities in the running of the denominational schools. These denominational boards were allowed to recommend persons for positions but a government authority carried out hiring and disciplinary actions. Denominational schools taught their particular religion and were not obliged to teach any other. Persons of a different religion can choose not to attend religious education classes. Students of all schools should now enjoy equal opportunities for placement in a secondary school via a common secondary school entrance examination.

The competitive College Exhibition Examination that catered for only few students was replaced by the Common Entrance Examination, which was available to all eleven and twelve year old children from 1961 onward. New secondary schools were built and secondary education was reorganised to cater to the academic, technical, general or practical needs of the students and the community (I.E.C., 1962; Gowrie, 1993; Keller, 1993). A technical School was built in Port of Spain. Scholarships and other assistance were given to qualifying persons to study at Universities and other institutions. Adult education classes, with the help of the government, catered to the education of adults who were so inclined (I.E.C., 1962).

The National Association for Retarded People started the Lady Hochoy Home and school in 1961 (M.Ed. Students, 1993).

In 1962, when Trinidad and Tobago became an independent nation, there were: -

· 90 government primary schools

· 346 assisted primary schools

· sixteen government secondary schools

· 21 assisted secondary schools

· one government special school

· ten assisted special schools (I.E.C., 1962)

1962 – 1999

Before 1961, education was never seen as an investment. The economic impact of giving people an education was not understood at the time. It was Theodore Shultz, the President of the U.S. Economic Association, who believed that investment in schooling would bring economic returns. So in 1962, the World Bank began to loan money for education purposes. A Commission of Enquiry into subversive activities was appointed in 1963 and UNESCO came to Trinidad and Tobago in that same year and drew up a plan for education. In 1965, the Industrial Stabilisation Act was brought about and in 1966, the Education Act came into being. In 1967, the Audrey Jeffers School for Deaf Children was opened by the Association in Aid of the Deaf and Dumb and in 1969, the National Association for Retarded Children opened their Gasparillo School. However by 1968, the UNESCO plan on education was in effect and in 1971, Junior Secondary Schools were opened (Keller, 1993). These schools were run on a double-shift system to cater for as many students as possible, with the aim of education for all (London, 1994). The plan here was to send one-third of the Junior Secondary School graduates to Senior Comprehensive Schools. In 1972, Servol was formed to cater for students who were having behaviour problems because of emotional difficulties. During the period from 1971 to 1974, there were consultations on education more than ever before. In 1973, OPEC countries set a common oil price, thus creating the oil boom. The Industrial Stabilisation Act of 1965 was changed to the Industrial Relations Act in 1974. This same year, the Senior Comprehensive Schools were not ready to accommodate the Junior Secondary School graduates so these children were placed in 'prestige' schools (Keller, 1993).

During the period 1975 to 1982, there were no consultations or planning in Education as a result of the oil boom. The World Bank plan was abandoned in 1975 because Trinidad and Tobago had lots of oil money and there were protests from parents about the Junior Secondary and Senior Comprehensive Schools, which were thought to be inferior in curriculum content. As a result, all students were sent to the same schools, from the Junior Secondary Schools to the Senior Comprehensive Schools. All students did Vocational, Technical and Academic Subjects. Social integration was thus encouraged.

Meanwhile, the National Association for Retarded Children (NARC) opened their school in the southern town of Penal in 1977 and in 1979, the year the Winchell Report made recommendations for developing special education, the Happy Haven Special School was opened in Tobago. One year later, N.A.R.C. opened the doors to Memisa in east Trinidad (M.Ed. Students, 1993).

1980 was also a major step in the development of Special Education in Trinidad and Tobago. Cabinet Minute No. 3901 of 1980 created a Special Education Unit in the Ministry of Education (M.Ed. Students, 1993). This unit was responsible for identifying children who needed special education and to determine their levels of need. They were also required to establish guidelines and supervision for all the special schools in the country in an attempt to raise the standard of education offered to the students, and to advise the Minister of Education on all matters pertaining to special education.

The St. Clair King Report of 1982 highlighted the need for remedial work and relevantly qualified teachers at the level of the Junior Secondary and Senior Comprehensive Schools. 1983 began the United Nations Decade of Disabled Persons with the UN producing guidelines for the treatment of and provisions for disabled persons. The Marge Report of 1984 sought to identify the number of disabled children and their disabilities. This Report recommended the '...*modification of existing structures...*' *(p. 31),* and went on to mention the

> '...*installation of ramps, elevators, appropriate bathroom fixtures and facilities, appropriate transportation and other changes.*' *(pp. 31,32)*

This led to the Education Plan of 1985 –1990.

In 1986, the National Association for Downes Syndrome (NADS) opened its school doors and in 1988, the government opened the Wharton Patrick School and the Point-a-Pierre Government

Special School. In 1989, the Macro-Economic Policy Medium Term (1989 – 1995) dealt with methods of dealing with the deficiencies of the students entering secondary schools, suggesting an increase in technical/vocational teachers and a change in the curriculum (ibid.).

Although the oil boom ended in 1979, economic and social adjustment did not begin until 1983 (Keller, 1993). Secondary education for all was not yet achieved and unsuccessful Common Entrance pupils were being neglected. A Post Primary Project, of which I was a working member, was piloted in 1988 in an attempt to cater to the educational needs of these students, in the absence of financial resources for constructing new secondary schools (London, 1994).

The Draft Policy Statement on Persons With Disabilities (1993) details suggested measures that should be taken to allow access for disabled persons. They begin with the need for legislation requiring new public buildings, including schools, to be accessible to all persons and recommends modification of educational institutes, hospitals and police stations and all other existing public buildings. The report also recommends the modification of an appropriate number of public transport vehicles and the provision of specific seats to accommodate disabled persons.

The Pilgrim Report (1990), a forerunner to the Draft Policy Statement on Persons With Disabilities (1993), made the same recommendations as the Draft Policy Statement on Persons With Disabilities (1993), but the Pilgrim Report included access to housing for disabled persons. Absent from all these reports, including the Education Policy Paper 1993 – 2003 (1993), is the need to alter playground facilities to allow the disabled child to participate in activities outside the classroom with non-disabled children.

In 1993, the Report of the National Task Force on Education was laid in Parliament. This report was produced by a team of nineteen educators, chaired by Carol Keller, the Dean of the Faculty of Education at the University of the West Indies at St. Augustine. The team accepted information and suggestions from educators and members of the public nationwide, before and after the report was laid in Parliament. The final report became the Education Policy Paper 1993 – 2003 and recommended curriculum goals, which take into consideration

> *The necessity to ensure that a programme of values education (multi-cultural sensitivities, aesthetic development, religious understanding, etc.) is a foundational element in the curriculum.'*
> *(p. xii)*

Unlike its predecessors, the Education Policy Paper 1993 – 2003 dedicated a section of its report specifically to Special Education.

This document, also referred to as the White Paper on Education, begins the Executive Summary with the following statement: -

> *'As a national community, we are fully committed to the view that <u>all</u> our citizens, regardless of their gender, class, culture, ethnic origin, etc, have the ability to learn and should be provided with the opportunity to develop that potential to the fullest.'* *(p. vii)*

Further in the text, The White Paper clearly states the beliefs that all children have *'...an inalienable right...'* *(p. xvii)* to education, and they all have *'...the ability to learn...'* *(ibid)*. The document further states that schools should provide for differences in abilities and offer opportunities for the development of individual talents. It is therefore clear that the Task Force and the nation are conscious of the need for education for all.

One of the major issues underlying this report is the ability of the learning systems to produce the type of results that should be expected for the amount of expenditure per student (ibid). In 1991, it was estimated that some 67.2% of children with special needs were in the mainstream primary and secondary schools with no special education provisions available to them (Keller et al, 1993). The White Paper found the system to be incapable of catering to children with special education needs and in early childhood education. This problem can be directly linked to a number of factors, including the following that are of direct concern to this study.

A lot of school buildings were built years ago and are in need of repairs. This was given as one reason for low teacher morale in the service. In addition, there is the absence of a method to continuously assess learning and diagnose problems in the system and of the learners.

The White Paper has therefore made recommendations, which include policy reforms and enabling policies with methods to broaden access and improve quality. In order to accomplish this, professional preparation and specialization of our education personnel was seen as one of the tasks we needed to work on. Pre-employment teacher preparation was seen as essential to the development and improvement of the teaching service. They recommended continuous professional development throughout the service of the educator for fulfilling the personal and professional needs of the educator and to enhance the quality of delivery and improve the efficiency of the system.

They also saw a need for mainstreaming children with special needs and converting special schools to centres for specialized services. It was proposed that children with severe special needs should continue to attend special schools with a view to eventual mainstreaming. To identify the difficulties being experienced by students so that remediation could be planned, to assist schools in providing for students with special needs and to educate the public on issues pertaining to disability, Diagnostic Prescriptive Centres were proposed for each of the eight education districts in the country. In the case of early detection of a condition, plans can be put in place to prevent difficulties. Care must be taken so that the testing does not become a labelling device, but is used so the teachers and parents can assist the children (Keller et al, 1993).

The White Paper also recommends that promotion be on a basis of achievement and not on age as still obtains at times in some of our schools. Students should show competencies at their present levels before being allowed to enter the next. To assist in creating a national norm for achievement levels, national tests were introduced at the end of Standard One and Standard Three. These tests, according to information gathered from six (6) primary schools in east Trinidad, are not properly administered and schools do not appear to be using the tests, as they should.

In accordance with the recommendations of the White Paper, the Common Entrance Examination, which was abolished in 2000, was replaced by the Secondary Entrance Assessment as a means for selection of students for the secondary schools. Junior Secondary Schools were de-shifted, new schools were built and existing schools were expanded to afford full secondary education for all students.

GLOBAL POLICIES

Human Rights

The United Nations recognises that equality is a fundamental requisite to 'freedom, justice and peace in the world.' In the absence of equality, 'freedom from fear and want' cannot be achieved. It is therefore necessary that human rights should be protected by law. In so doing, a better standard of living can be achieved. Member states have therefore

> '...pledged themselves to achieve...the promotion of universal respect for and observance of human rights and fundamental freedoms.' (Preamble, UN Declaration of Human Rights, 1948)

> 'The General Assembly proclaims this Universal Declaration of Human Rights as a common standard of achievement for all peoples and all nations...' (United Nations General Assembly, 1948)

Though this Universal Declaration did not become law then, in 1966 the International Covenant on Civil and Political Rights and the International Covenant on Economic, Social and Cultural rights, were unanimously adopted, thereby making the provisions of the Universal Declaration binding and legal.

'All Peoples' refers to all human beings of any creed, race, nationality, colour, sex, language, religion, political or other opinion, or ability.

Article 1 of the UN Declaration on Human Rights states,

'All human beings are born free and equal in dignity and rights. They are endowed with reason and conscience and should act towards one another in a spirit of brotherhood.' (UNGA)

We are all formed from one human sperm and one human ovum, making us 100% human babies. If, for some reason, we are born with an impairment, this does not change the fact that we were formed from human gametes. We are still human. If we acquire an impairment because of some accident or abuse, we remain human beings. Therefore, the first principle is the recognition that disabled persons are human beings. All human beings, including disabled persons are born free and equal in dignity and rights.

Reason and conscience are two properties of the human person, which can be at different abilities for different individuals. Each individual is unique. We therefore have different levels of reason and conscience. Nevertheless, we should act towards other human beings in a spirit of brotherhood or sisterhood.

Article 2 specifies that everyone of all races, colours, sexes, languages, religions, political or other opinions, national or social origins, properties, birth or other status, is entitled to these rights and freedoms stated in this Declaration. That right remains, even if that person is imprisoned or disabled.

Article 3 ensures *'the right to life, liberty and security of person.'* (UNCHR) to everyone, including disabled persons, while Article 6 ensures *'...the right to recognition...as a person.'* Disabled persons must be recognised as persons who have rights, and these rights recognised as being equal in every sense. Article 7 further confirms that

'All are equal before the law and are entitled without any discrimination to equal protection of the law.'

Article 12 states

'No one shall be subjected to arbitrary interference with his privacy, family, home or correspondence, nor to attacks upon his honour and reputation.'

Disabled persons and their parents/guardians have the right to refuse any intrusion by persons who take charge of their lives, without being asked.

The United Nations recognises a child as anyone below the age of eighteen or the age of majority recognised by individual countries. If a country's age of majority is sixteen, then a person under sixteen years old is recognised as a child. The sixteen-year-old is considered an adult and is expected to be treated as such in accordance with the Declaration on Human Rights. (Article 1)

The Rights of the Child

Some of the articles of the UN Declaration on Human Rights can be applied to children. However, it was thought necessary to identify specific rights for all children.

The United Nations Declaration on the Rights of the Child was unanimously adopted by the United Nations General Assembly in 1959. This Declaration set out ten principles, which state firmly, that children must be afforded the best treatment that mankind has to give. The Declaration states that children have a right to a home and a nationality. They must also, as a matter of right, have access to, and receive health care, education, rest and play, even if they are disabled and/or orphaned. Children also have a right to be protected from separation from parents, all types of exploitation, abuse and engagement in warfare. The right to be heard on decisions affecting their lives and, as they become more matured, increasing opportunities to take part in activities of society, are rights which ensure participation in life.

This Declaration and the Declaration of Human Rights have guided the way children worldwide have been treated for 31 years. In September 1990, the Convention on the Rights of the Child, which began drafting in the International Year of the Child, 1979, became international law. In 1993, the UN Standard Rules on the Equalisation of Opportunities for Persons with Disabilities stated international standards for the making of policies and follow-up action concerning disabled people. The next year, 1994, saw a report from UNESCO calling for all countries to implement the inclusive approach to education of all children. This report, masterminded by more than 300 participants representing 92 governments and 25 international organisations, is known as The Salamanca Statement and the Framework for Action on Special Needs Education, 1994. This document is the most comprehensive international document produced with worldwide consensus on special education and education as a whole.

The participants were not just government officials and United Nations representatives.

> '...the Conference brought together senior education officials, administrators, policymakers and specialists, as well as representatives of the United Nations and the Specialised Agencies, other international governmental organisations, non-governmental organisations and donor agencies.' (Federico Mayor, Preface, Salamanca Statement, 1994; p.iii.)

This means that persons actually involved in special education were part of the decision making process.

The UN Convention on the Rights of the Child (1989) states in Article 28 that children have a right to education and that this education must be on the basis of equal opportunity for all children. The 1989 Convention's Article 29 states that the child's education should develop mental and physical abilities, talents and personality to its fullest. When doing so, we should remember that each child's characteristics, interests, and abilities and needs are unique and we should take these into account. In addition, support services must be readily accessible to all disabled students.

The UN Standard Rules on the Equalisation of Opportunities for Persons with Disabilities (1993) agree that every child has a basic right to education but the UN Standard Rules 6 further states:

> *'Countries should recognise the principle of equal primary, secondary and tertiary educational opportunities for children, youth and adults with disabilities, in integrated settings.' (CSIE, 1995; section 3)*

In the Proclamation, the delegates at Salamanca, Spain stated their beliefs in the fundamental right to education to every child. They also believe that opportunities must be given so that the child would

> *'...achieve and maintain an acceptable level of learning...' (Salamanca Statement, 1994; p. iii.)*

More specifically, the Statement recognises the right of disabled persons to express their wishes on education and the rights of parents to be consulted on the type of education best suited to their individual child(ren).

In reaffirming their commitment to *Education for All*, the delegates recognised the need for inclusive education and encouraged its implementation in the Framework for Action on Special Needs Education. The Framework proposes that all children be accommodated in all schools.

> 'This should include disabled and gifted children, street and working children, children from remote or nomadic populations, children from linguistic, ethnic or cultural minorities and children from other disadvantaged or marginalized areas or groups.''
> (The Salamanca Statement, p. 6.)

Many children experience some form of learning difficulty at some time in their lives and therefore schools must be prepared to accommodate them. They should therefore be prepared to cater for children with serious disabilities with a child-centred curriculum capable of educating all students successfully. The curriculum should be adapted to suit the needs of the students. Children with special needs should receive support within the regular curriculum. They should not be taught using a different curriculum because all children should be provided with the same education.

Formative evaluation should be used in order to track the progress of both teacher effectiveness and student progress. Any weaknesses can be thus identified and appropriate steps taken to overcome them. Special education needs can be catered for by use of learning aids in the form of teaching strategy, equipment or specialist teachers. The Framework suggests a central pool for supplying '...appropriate and affordable technology.' (Salamanca Statement, 1994; p.23). Such an inclusive school can encourage and lead to an inclusive community.

> *'Child centred schools are, moreover, the training ground for a people-oriented society that respects both the differences and the dignity of all human beings.' (The Salamanca Statement, 1994; p. 7)*

In an inclusive school, children learn with their peers, in spite of differences and difficulties. Those who have special education needs receive support services to aid learning. But in order to be successful, inclusive schools need committed efforts by teachers and other school staff, parents, volunteers and community. The Framework for Action advised that special schools should act as resource centres for ordinary schools, which will actually be inclusive schools. Teacher training institutions and special schools should act as resources for assistive technology equipment and their operations as well as training in instructional strategies. Support services can be tapped from other agencies or government bodies like social services and health.

Article 23 of the UN Convention on the Rights of the Child states the right of disabled children to enjoy full and decent lives in dignity. Conditions should promote self-reliance and ensure access to active community participation (CSIE 1995, Section 2). This means that recreation, healthcare and rehabilitation, employment preparation, training and education should be all accessible to all children.

The Salamanca Statement 1994, in its Framework for Action, calls upon governments to pass laws enabling inclusion in all schools, except in extreme cases of disability. In its guidelines, the Framework stated that legislation should include the fields of health, social welfare, vocational training and employment in order to have any effect in education.

Legislation should be specific about children attending their neighbourhood schools with the exception of special cases where the child's education would be better met in a special school. However, part-time attendance at regular schools for these special classes should be encouraged.

Legislation should also pay particular attention to girls and women with disabilities and persons with multiple disabilities, ensuring equal access and equal opportunities. The Salamanca Statement (1994) considers girls' education a priority area. A disabled girl has a double disadvantage in many parts of the world. Special programmes should be implemented to provide accessible information and guidance to these children.

Sign language should be recognised as the official means of communication of deaf persons and so priority should be given to this in the education of deaf persons.

Funds for improvements in the education systems should be given priority to enable early childhood education, girls' education and teacher education. Early childhood education is necessary to develop a readiness for inclusive education. Early identification and assessment mean the potential for early implementation of intervention strategies, leading to all-round preparation for school. At this level, inclusion becomes natural to students and the transition to primary school is automatic.

Quite a number of reasons are given against the idea of inclusive education, but one of the foremost hindrances to inclusion is teachers' attitude towards disability and their expectations of disabled students. Clough and Lindsay (1991) explained that teachers' attitudes to inclusion are affected by a number of factors. Their concept of special needs may be limited to include only those persons with severe or profound impairments. Children with mild and moderate learning difficulties would not be recognized as children with special education needs.

Research done by Bowman in 1989 revealed that about 25% of teachers interviewed are in favour of integrating children with physical and mental conditions, but only about 10% agreed with integration of those with severe mental and multiple conditions (Clough and Lindsay, 1991). Of the fourteen surveyed, those teachers who were from countries with laws requiring integration were more in favour of integration. This seems to suggest that laws should be passed and enforced, requiring compulsory mainstreaming of all pupils of students age in Trinidad and Tobago.

The Ward and Centre study in Australia revealed that the teachers were more concerned with the pupils' behaviour rather than the type of disability the children had. This report also suggests that disabilities were grouped according to demands the teacher saw the disability would have on their time and extra skills that would be needed to deal with the disabilities.

School administrators are responsible for creating a positive attitude and effective co-operation among team members. Through consultation and negotiation, the administrators identify the exact roles of the partners in the education process. Since the success of the child is the responsibility of all partners, the school as a whole should take responsibility for the education of special needs children. Partners and volunteers should also be invited to assist the school.

Governments should ensure that teacher education provide training for special needs education in inclusive schools. In the Framework for Action, the Salamanca Statement (1994) sets out guidelines for the 'Recruitment and Training of Education Personnel'. It states that teachers and other education personnel should be trained to cater for special education needs in the classroom.

> *The knowledge and skills required are mainly those of good teaching and include assessing special needs, adapting curriculum content, utilising assistive technology, individualising teaching procedures to suit a larger range of abilities, etc.'* (Salamanca Statement, 1994; p. 27)

All teachers in an inclusive setting need to possess these skills and knowledge. Managers should therefore ensure pre-service education for all new teachers and in-service updates and re-training for new and existing teachers. Pilgrim (1990) and Keller et al (1993) recommended this type of training and further recommended the setting up of degree courses in Special Education at the University of the West Indies so that more teachers can avail themselves of the programmes.

An inclusive setting should also include disabled teachers. The Framework for Action suggests recruiting of qualified, disabled teachers and school personnel to work in inclusive settings. Disabled students would strive for success if they have successful role models who are disabled.

Collaboration with other agencies like Teacher Associations and Universities with more experience in Special Education provisions is encouraged. The Statement calls on non-governmental organisations to be more involved with official national bodies in the

'...planning, implementation and evaluation of inclusive provision for special educational needs...' (Salamanca Statement, 1994; p.xi).

The Statement further calls on UNESCO, as the international education agency, to include special needs education as part of all discussions on education for all, and to encourage teachers' associations to support special education training for members. This initiative was taken by teachers and the Trinidad and Tobago Unified Teachers' Association long before the Salamanca Statement (1994) suggested this. Contact was made with the University of the West Indies who saw no need for such a programme, and then with University of Sheffield. The latter, in association with TTUTA, began a programme, which by 1995 educated some 60 teachers at the certificate, diploma and masters level in Special Education. Unfortunately, according to the contents of a letter written to me in 1997, the Ministry of Education refused to acknowledge these qualifications that are highly regarded internationally.

The Framework for Action also encouraged participation of parents/guardians, community and special interest groups and even exchanges with countries with experience in inclusive education.

UNESCO was also asked to encourage research, networking and the establishment of regional centres to serve as sources of information. The Framework proposes the establishment of centres from which research information and findings can be disseminated on a national level. It also suggests the integration of special needs education in research institutes and curriculum development centres with special attention being paid to *'...action research focusing on innovative teaching-learning strategies.'* (The Salamanca Statement; p. 24-25). It advocates the active participation of classroom teachers and the launching of pilot experiments and in-dept studies for future action.

Staff in special schools has the expertise for early identification and intervention. Special schools can also serve as training institutions for mainstream teachers and as a resource centres for the specific disability they serve. For example, the Cascade School for the Deaf conducts classes in Sign Language for the public. These classes were initially set up for parents and other relatives of deaf students and for interested teachers of mainstream schools. They have expanded to include police, court and hospital officials and interested members of the public. Unfortunately, these people fund their own education, resulting in few persons actually taking advantage of classes.

In countries with few special schools in remote or rural areas, a large number of special education needs students are not catered for. Efforts should be concentrated on establishing inclusive schools in these areas. The Salamanca Statement (1994) states that priority should also be given to preparation for adult life and adult and continuing education. The different agencies and services involved in adult life should get together to assist schools in preparing young, disabled people for adult life. An effective school-to-work transition is necessary for all students moving from the school's protective environment to the hectic world of work or higher education. An appropriate curriculum in transition skills is therefore necessary so that all students can have practical experience in various settings prior to graduating from secondary education. Adult education classes should also be established. Special attention and priority should be given to persons with disabilities who want to attend these classes. Courses should be designed to accommodate adult students with different categories of disabilities. Special attention should be paid to disabled women.

This Framework proposes community based rehabilitation, led by persons with disabilities and their families, combined with communities and other education, health, vocational and welfare services. Barriers to inclusion will thus be removed and progress monitored using continuous assessment.

The Salamanca Statement calls on governments with international programmes and funding agencies to promote inclusive education as part of all education programmes. It also calls on the United Nations agencies, especially the International Labour Office (ILO), the World Health Organisation (WHO), UNESCO and UNICEF to co-operate more in an effort to expand the integration of special needs students in all education systems.

The Salamanca Statement sees inclusion as a means of eliminating discrimination and building an inclusive society while improving efficiency in education. It requires countries to implement practical plans towards inclusion in all schools. This involves placing high priority on budget allocations for education and creating legislation to ensure implementation of inclusive practices. The Framework for Action suggests that since special education is successfully used to teach children with difficulties and/or disabilities, then all children should be able to learn using this method. Schools should therefore be prepared for inclusion by being able to recognise and respond to differences in students' abilities.

Member countries are expected to respect the rights of all children and to ensure these rights are afforded to all children, as Article 2 (1) of the Convention on the Rights of the Child states: -

> '...*within their jurisdiction without discrimination of any kind, irrespective of the child's or his or her parent's or legal guardian's race, colour, sex, language, religion, political or other opinion, national, ethnic or social origin, property, disability, birth or other status.*'

This responsibility for ensuring these rights and the protection of the child from discrimination or punishment because of disability, is the expressed responsibility of each member country. This means that society is legally accountable for meeting the obligations of the Convention.

> '*States shall ensure that each child enjoys full rights without discrimination or distinction of any kind.*' *(UNHRC, 1990.)*

Article 13 (1) of the Declaration of Human Rights tells that '*Everyone has the right to freedom of movement and residence within the borders of each state.*' In addition, '*Everyone has a right to freedom of opinion and expression...*' *(Article 19, ibid)* and '*Everyone has the right of equal access to public service in his country.*' *(Article 21 (2), ibid)*. This means that a disabled child and his/her parents/guardians have the right to choose for that child to live at home with his/her parents and siblings while attending school. They can also choose for that child to travel to his/her respective school, using a choice of public service transport or personal transport. The child, with the parents' help, can decide not to live at school, without fear of any punishment and with the expectation of receiving what is due to him/her as a human being with equal rights. Vasey (1994) describes her experiences of disability as being lonely and frustrating at times. During the earlier periods of her life, her experiences seemed to be limited to the immediate family and neighbourhood. Her parents assisted her with daily activities and she worked in the immediate environs. With the expansion of services of disabled persons, she was able to move on to a wider territory and so expand her experiences.

> 'Everyone has a right to education. Education shall be free, at least in the elementary and fundamental stages. Elementary education shall be compulsory.' (Article 26 (1), UN Declaration of Human Rights)

All children including disabled children have this right to free education.

Article 26 (2) (ibid) states: -

> 'Education shall be directed to the full development of the human personality and to the strengthening of respect for human rights and fundamental freedoms. It shall promote understanding, tolerance and friendship among all nations, racial or religious groups...'

For full development of the human personality, an all-round education is needed. This will include all curriculum areas, including the hidden curriculum. Therefore it would be necessary for disabled children to attend school with their non-disabled counterparts. To 'promote understanding, tolerance and friendship among all nations, racial or religious groups...' (ibid) we must use early intervention and educate children, disabled and non-disabled, in the same classroom, as far as possible. This way, they grow together to understand and tolerate in friendship and take these qualities to the wider world (Salamanca Statement, 1994).

Article 26 (3) of the UN Declaration of Human Rights states: -

'Parents have a prior right to choose the kind of education that shall be given to their children.' They should be therefore allowed to send their child(ren) to the school(s) of their choice.

> *'In all actions concerning children,…the best interest of the child shall be a primary consideration.'* (Article 3, UN Convention on the Rights of the Child)

Schools should therefore be structured so that the best interest of the child will be served. This means a well-structured education system should be set up with appropriate legislation for the implementation of practices by competent administrators and proficient classroom teachers.

Article 4 (ibid) expects states to do all in their power, and as far as their resources permit, to ensure that these rights stated in this Convention, are adhered to. The international body is expected to assist countries that are unable to implement basic rights.

Article 5 states that the responsibilities, the rights and the duties of parents, guardians, extended family, community family or any person or persons responsible for the child, are to be respected (ibid).

Article 7 should be given special note because it, in part, speaks for the many students housed in dormitories at residential schools. It states that the child shall have *'…the right to know and be cared for by his or her parents' (ibid)*. Again, it is the responsibility of the country's government to pass laws using these international guidelines. However, children have to be taken from their homes at an early age to live at the school for deaf children to be educated. The majority of their young lives are spent with workers who change shifts and their teachers. This is surely not what children want.

Article 15 recognises the right of the child to freely associate and peacefully assemble. Under the living arrangements of the school for deaf children, peaceful assembly with fellow students outside the dorm is possible but what about free association? These students cannot associate with whom they want since they are unable to meet with their peers in their hometowns or neighbourhood school or playground.

The right to education is included here so if the person has an impairment, this does not change the fact that he/she is a person and he/she has rights. Further, the Convention states: -

> 'Disabled children shall have the right to special treatment, education and care. Primary education shall be free and compulsory as early as possible.' (UNHCR, 1990.)

This researcher believes that in order to have primary education available to all children as early as possible, it is necessary to have ample school places available, with sufficient, well-trained teachers ready to take the responsibility of educating the children. Education is a right of the disabled child and he/she should therefore be accepted at any school that the parent chooses. The disabled child should not be refused admission on the grounds of the school not having the capable or trained personnel. These personnel should be provided. In addition, if primary education is to begin as early as possible, an organised pre-school system should be established. In this way, children would be prepared from an early age, to enter the mainstream education classroom. Further, it would be possible to identify any possible signs of disability from an earlier age so that intervention can begin in infancy. With the right caregivers, children at risk would have a better chance of coping with and completing their formal primary education.

SOME EXPERIENCES OF DISABLED PEOPLE

Disabled people are in a constant struggle for survival. Pre-natal testing of mother and foetus are common in today's world. The foetus, if found to be unfit, could be recommended for termination. This eliminates the possibility of any disabled babies being born. The expectant mother, in her ignorance, is likely to take the advice of the professional.

If the baby survives the womb and the parent is told that the child is born with impairment, the accompanying actions of the medical professionals communicate a feeling of bereavement and isolation. The parent is made to feel that a child was lost in the birth process.

Parents are not warned of the oppression and the anxiety that lie ahead. They are not encouraged to feel proud of the disabled child. Society therefore denies the basic human rights of disabled children. Parents sometimes spend so much time fighting for the child there is no time or energy left '...*to play and have fun with their children.*' *(Mason 1994, p. 3)*

When parents are stressed and unhappy, the child here may feel guilty about 'causing' the problems of the parents. This son or daughter may feel that he/she must co-operate in order to receive love from parents or caregivers. The child will eventually find himself/herself in a strange world that sees him/her as a person with impairment(s).

> '...the child is like any other, driven to learn and become itself – a whole, new person with a body, mind and soul.' (Mason 1994, p. 4)

Through self motivation, the disabled child tries to gain control of his/her life and develops a personality through interactions with others. Positive interactions with others help the child learn co-operation and confidence. Intervention strategies utilised by professionals and service providers destroy any natural relationships that may be formed between disabled persons and others, including parents and siblings.

Since therapy is the adult's method of personal and physical development, the child does not play and develop as children are meant to grow. *'Play is about the child's goals, therapy is about the adult's goals.'* (Mason 1994, p. 4)

Vasey (1994) writes about her struggles for her right to live in a world that viewed her as a burden to society.

> *'It is not easy to function in a society that does not accommodate wheelchair users on public transport'* (Vasey 1994, p.4).

She noted the joy she experienced when at twenty-two years old she went out on her own for the first time. With this came the ever-present Personal Assistant who was not always welcome when personal relationships flourished. She seems to be content with her mobility now and takes into consideration the lifestyles of the general population, many of who may be unemployed and unable to get around as she does.

Vasey writes about personal assistants:

'Like a wheelchair, a sign language interpreter or a guide dog they form part of the solution to access barriers, but they also contribute to making disabled people different.' (Vasey, p. 12)

In any society, any group that is in the minority is considered different. So, disabled people would be considered different. A personal assistant or aid only makes the difference obvious.

Mike Oliver (1994) suggests that language is used by non-disabled people to communicate domination and control of disabled people by non-disabled people. Labels are therefore used to categorise people, making it

'...easier for us as a society to lock them up, drug them into insensibility, electrocute or even kill them.' (Oliver 1994, p. 5)

So, according to Oliver (1994), the language of policy, written by non-disabled persons, spell service to people who are unable to care for themselves. This implies that disabled people benefit from welfare programmes set up by non-disabled people and disabled children benefit from special education programmes set up by non-disabled persons. In addition, the rights of disabled persons depend on the language of policies set up by non-disabled persons (ibid). This researcher agrees with Oliver and believes that segregated provisions in education deny the rights of disabled children just as people of African descent and Africans were denied their rights in pre-civil rights America or Apartheid run South Africa respectively.

Fulcher (1989) theorises that the category of disability is used by welfare states to control citizens. She notes that the category itself is disputed since there is no clear definition and no accurate measure of degree of disability. She also notes that doctors may be biased in their judgements. Social institutions, including educational institutions, reveal biases also. The majority of special education needs students have no known impairment. The presumption is made that there is an impairment (ibid). This places a blame on the students for not performing well when

> *'An alternative politics would locate deficits in school practices, particularly in curriculum and pedagogical practices. (ibid, p. 25)*

Fulcher (1989) also describes disability as a personal tragedy seen by society as a personal trouble that should be contained. Distribution of benefits is a means of ensuring that it remains a private matter and not become a public issue. Again, students with special needs are labelled as disabled and having personal problems and curriculum issues are ignored.

In Trinidad and Tobago, I spoke to three persons I know about their experiences of disability. It is interesting to know that all three shared the same wishes – that disabled people be treated with the same respect that non-disabled people receive. In the following accounts, I have not used real names.

Nine year old Kewin was a lively, intelligent Standard Three student who was always anxious to complete his assignments. He was from a close-knit family of two boys and one girl from a rural village in Central Trinidad. Following the Christmas vacation, Kewin returned to my class less active than before. He began to complain of pains in his right ear. His father, a single parent, was financially unable to immediately cater for his eldest son's medical care. The condition therefore progressed, rendering Kewin profoundly deaf within the year. There were no teachers qualified to teach Kewin at our school and the students were able to communicate with him better than the teachers. The then principal of a school for deaf children visited our school at the request of a senior teacher. As a qualified audiologist, he tested Kewin and offered to enrol him at the school for deaf children. However, there was a waiting list. In addition, Kewin's father was unable to finance his son's move to a residential school some 50 miles away from home. After paying for his accommodation at the school he would not be able to visit him or bring him home on weekends.

Kewin could not continue his education and became dependent on others. Eight years later, he told me how frustrating and embarrassing it was and still is for him. He still has problems communicating with his neighbours and is unable to communicate with other deaf persons because of his lack of knowledge of sign language.

Sharon, a friendly secondary school student who was eager to learn, was accepted by her friends as one of the girls. She was a normally energetic adolescent who enjoyed life. Her greatest problem, however, was access. Improvements to the secondary school she attended were limited to ramps on the ground floor of the buildings. Doorknobs were never adjusted and the tension on these doors remained the same. She needed assistance to go through doors. The restrooms could not accommodate wheelchairs so she always needed assistance to use them. Her studies too depended on her peers' availability and willingness. She had to be lifted and taken to the upper floor while a peer would bring up her wheelchair. This was the only way to access the library. In her frustration one afternoon, with tears in her eyes, she told one of her teachers, "I feel as though I'm not wanted here." She said she feels that she is a burden to her peers, and a burden to society.

When Stephanie, a caring motivator and classroom assistant applied to pursue the certificate in Early Childhood Education at the university, she indicated that she was deaf. Stephanie attended an interview with a sign language interpreter and was accepted. She enrolled and began attending classes. Stephanie was born deaf and learnt to rely heavily on lip reading and sign language. She attended classes with a friend, an interpreter, who was of great help. However, her friend was not always able to be present. In the interpreter's absence, one lecturer was able to adjust his style to allow Stephanie to see his face at all times when he was lecturing. He would also repeat questions posed to him so that she could see what was asked. The others stood against the glare of the windows, spoke with their backs towards her and obscured the plain view of their faces. Stephanie told me that she was totally confused, lost and unable to participate in any class actively. It took a long time for her to catch up. She became very reluctant to pursue any further studies. Stephanie was a very good assistant and would be a great teacher if given the opportunity.

These are just three of the many cases I have seen unfolding over the years. Because of our history of dominance for many years by the medical model of disability, our education system is designed to cater for non-disabled children, while, as the education Act of 1966 states, the Minister *may* cause the establishment of special schools. In spite of all the fancy language of the consultations and their recommendations for education, the education act remains the law. There has been no attempt to change this act. In Trinidad and Tobago we need to firstly change many of our laws so that our signatures on international policies and statements like the United Nations Convention on the Rights of the Child and the Salamanca Statement would have meaning for us here at home.

Chapter 3

Methodology

RESEARCH DESIGN

B ell (1993) describes research as *a 'systematic approach'* and quotes Howard and Sharp's (1983) definition of research as:

> *'...seeking through methodical processes to add to one's own body of knowledge and, hopefully, to that of others, by the discovery of non-trivial fact and insights.' (p. 2)*

Cohen and Manion (1994) cites Mouly's (1978) definition of research as:

> *'...the process of arriving at dependable solutions to problems through the planned and systematic collection, analysis, and interpretation of data.' (p. 40)*

According to Cohen and Manion (1994), quantitative research is *'...directed at analysing the relationship and regularities between selected factors...' (p. 7),* while Bell (1993) says, *'Quantitative research collects facts and study the relationship of one set of facts to another.' (p. 5).* Quantitative research therefore, deals with statistics. On the other hand, qualitative research is '...*more concerned to understand individuals' perceptions of the world.' (ibid. p. 6)* and therefore uses methods that are concerned with quality and meaning.

This research combines both quantitative and qualitative methods because in educational research, we cannot rely solely on statistics and ignore the perceptions of the individuals who are the key players in the largely human system.

This research, like the majority of education research, can be viewed as being descriptive since it deals with

> '...*conditions or relationships that exist; practices that prevail; beliefs, points of views, or attitudes that are held; processes that are going on; effects that are being felt; or trends that are developing.' (Cohen and Manion, 1994; p. 67, quoting Best, 1970)*

Barnes and Mercer (1997) state that disability research before the 1980's focussed on the individual's impairment. This they attribute to the fact that the medical model of disability was so dominant for so long before that researchers were unwilling to challenge the existing social structures or their professions. Organisations controlled and run by disabled persons reaffirmed their conviction that the medical model was oppressive and redefined disability as being caused by social organisations. Still, researchers stuck to the medical model for conducting social research.

The later 1980's saw a change towards research on experiences of disability and a move towards anti-discrimination legislation. Other oppressed groups joined and confirmed the belief by disabled activists that existing research was being used to exploit them. Disability research had to be completely separated from the mainstream approaches.

Oliver (1997) believes that

'...it is not possible to research oppression in an objective and scientific way' (p. 17).

He agrees with Barnes (1996), whom Oliver says argued that the researcher must take sides when doing research on oppression.

Emancipatory research is research condemning social oppression at all levels and facilitating change towards a better life for the oppressed. Research cannot be considered truly emancipatory unless it is used for this purpose or it contributes to emancipation of disabled people (ibid.). This researcher therefore agrees that in doing emancipatory research, the researcher must be on the side of the oppressed.

Emancipatory research rejects the idea of the researcher as expert with power to control

'...the design, implementation, analysis and dissemination of research findings' (Barnes and Mercer, 1997, p. 6).

The researched must be treated as experts who experience disability and must be represented by the researcher.

Emancipatory research *'...must be reflective and self-critical...'* *(ibid.)* in order to be effective as a tool to be used for the benefit of the researched.

In conducting the majority of the study from the United States, it was necessary to use the survey method of gathering data. The instruments were designed to obtain information in the following manner:

Data Type	Source of Information
Quantitative	Selected questions on the teachers' questionnaire
Qualitative	Selected questions on the teachers' questionnaire. Informal interviews with teachers.

The research questions are linked to the methodology in the following way:

Question	Research Question	Method of Collecting Information
1	Are special schools sufficiently prepared to offer an equal chance to students with special needs?	Quantitative data to be obtained from demographic questions and questions 1, 2 and 3. Qualitative data to be obtained from questions 4 through 11. Informal interviews with teachers.
2	How do teacher expectations of disabled students in special schools affect the content delivery?	Qualitative data to be obtained from questions 4 through 11.

SITE SELECTION

This research sought to investigate if the rights of special students were being infringed. This researcher decided to direct the investigation towards the special schools. In addition, the Schools Supervisor for Special Education in Trinidad and Tobago told me that there was no existing data about disabled children in mainstream schools.

The schools targeted for this research were special schools in the north of Trinidad. These schools constitute the majority of the special school population in the country. They include

· One school for deaf children

- One school for children with emotional and behavioural difficulties
- One school for blind children
- One school for physically challenged children
- Two schools for intellectually challenged children.

These schools cater for disabilities across categories, ages from 3½ years old to eighteen years old and both sexes.

PARTICIPANT SELECTION

The participants at these schools included teachers, without regard to experience. Their qualifications also vary from Teacher's Diploma to graduate degrees.

Because people with disabilities experience so many forms of violations against their rights as citizens and human beings, it is possible that they may not be able to identify abuses against themselves when these abuses occur (Rioux, Crawford, Ticoll and Bach, 1997). They may interpret abuse as normal interactions between and among human beings. It was therefore necessary, for the purpose of my research, to interpret their experiences from the perspective of others, their teachers. As far as possible, a dimensional sample was selected so that the schools and students would be proportionally represented. However, I attempted to structure my questionnaire so as not to establish my framework as a dominant one.

THE ROLE OF THE RESEARCHER

This researcher submitted an application to the Ministry of Education, requesting permission to conduct research in schools in Trinidad and Tobago. Meanwhile, I set about collecting relevant literature from the newspapers and magazines available to me. During my literature search, I found that research on human rights in education was non-existent in the country, except for the recommendations made in the Pilgrim Report (1984) and the White Paper (1993).

Reading through Chapter 18 of Equality and Diversity in Education 2, I noted that:

> '...*undertaking research within your employing institution raised a complex range of issues, such as loyalty, integrity and the position of power held by the researcher.' (Brock, 1995; p. 189)*

Immediately, I thought of my research topic and my position as an employee of the Ministry of Education and understood why this type of research is lacking in Trinidad and Tobago. Should I discover evidence of human rights violations, where should my loyalties lie? Should it be with my employer or with the victims of these violations? Should I compromise my integrity? Should I compromise my findings in an attempt to remain unscathed within the education system? Or should I use my power as a researcher, stand by my belief in human rights for all and expose any injustices that may exist at the expense of being disloyal towards my employer? Most people's loyalties seem to be with their employer. However I decided to disclose exactly what I find and state my conclusions and recommendations and proceed with the dissemination of my research findings.

In any case, I decided to proceed with my research. I planned on using a sample population of mainstream students with special education needs and students in special schools. In a conversation with the Schools Supervisor in charge of the Special Education Unit of the Ministry of Education, I requested a list of students in mainstream schools who had been referred to special schools for one reason or another, but are still on the waiting list because of lack of space or the commuting distance or any other reason. If such a list was not available to me because of legal issues, I would have been satisfied with a list of schools and the number of referred from each school listed. The Schools Supervisor informed me that there is no waiting list. He further said that it is a known fact that there is a 15% - 20% student population out there that has some form of disability but they have not been identified. He said that they remain undetected and hidden in the system. Maybe this can be another research idea. Why do these children remain undetected? What can be done to ensure that their disabilities are discovered, that they are assessed and that they are catered for according to the articles of the Convention on the Rights of the Child?

In light of this information, I decided to change the focus of my research to students in special schools. But before I could do any data gathering, I needed permission from the Ministry of Education. I had applied more than four months earlier to conduct research at the schools and had not yet received the approval. The Schools Supervisor informed me that he approved and signed my application and forwarded it to the relevant section of the Ministry. This was in late September. He informed me of the date the application left his office and showed me the official entry in the Unit's log. The application could not be traced. The Schools Supervisor apologised and asked me to resubmit an application directly to him and he would take care of it.

The day after my conversation with the Schools Supervisor, I travelled to the United States where I attempted to continue my research. Because I was not able to travel with all of my research material, my study suffered immensely. I came to the U. S. with only three texts on methodology and research methods. I had problems with retrieving all of my literature, especially newspaper and magazine clippings. Even with the use of the Internet, there was a lack of information on special education in Trinidad and Tobago. I remained with very little to work with and no support for a very long time. Sometimes I felt as if I was reading irrelevant material. I was still not sure how much notes I should take or what I should note. I recalled that it was better to take irrelevant notes with the important ones but then this seemed to be wasting a lot of time. Without the newspaper clippings and the copy of the White Paper on Education (1993 – 2003), it seeded impossible to successfully complete this task. My schedule was very inconsistent.

Almost three years after speaking to the schools supervisor, and with the help of a relative in Trinidad, I was able to obtain the necessary permission to conduct research. After piloting my questionnaire and completing it, I was assisted by a doctoral candidate in Education to distribute the questionnaires to teachers at the special schools mentioned previously in this chapter. He returned a few days later to collect the responses and brought them back to the United States, where he mailed them to me. Of the 35 questionnaires distributed, 32 were returned completed.

Data collected were tallied and coded to produce tables and graphs for easy reference. Qualitative information gathered from the questionnaire and from informal interviews with teachers, were analysed and discussed.

When the analysis and presentation of data were completed, conclusions were drawn and recommendations made in an attempt to improve any perceived shortcomings.

DATA COLLECTION AND DATA SOURCES

The survey questionnaire was prepared in an attempt to obtain both qualitative and quantitative data. Cohen and Manion (1994) suggested the use of elicited information along with supplied information since the supplied information may be irrelevant in some cases and the elicited may be important but sometimes overlooked. The open-ended questions sought to elicit qualitative data affecting students with disabilities. It is hoped that the responses were honest and not guided by personal constructs or organisational influences.

The questionnaire was typed and carried a cover letter, assuring teachers of anonymity and the availability of the research for their inspection. There were eleven questions, which were preceded by statistical data requesting the sex, age, level of formal preparation in Special Education, the number of years in teaching and the number of years at the present school. This information could be used to determine if there were any relationships among sex, age and commitment to teaching of students with special needs.

Informal interviews were also held with four teachers who are current in the system. Two of these teachers earned graduate degrees in Special Education and work at mainstream primary school and one is a Technical-Vocational Teacher at a mainstream secondary school.

The fourth is a lecturer of education at a teachers college. Though I have worked in schools in Trinidad and Tobago for more than seventeen (years, a lot of development took place since the genesis of this research one year before, and during my absence of approximately three years. These interviews were conducted in person in three cases and one was a virtual meeting.

ANALYSIS OF DATA

In analysing the questionnaire, the questions were categorised in the following manner: -

· Questions 1 – 3 sought to determine what physical adaptations and aids are used at the schools and if the teachers are sufficiently trained in the use of the aids.

· Questions 4 – 7 dealt with the application of the syllabus. They attempted to determine if the adaptations, if any, are appropriate for the delivery of the curriculum. They also told if teachers expect their students to do well and perform at the appropriate level.

· Questions 8 – 10 looked at the views of the teachers and their schools on mainstreaming. This gave an idea of how teachers expect the students to perform in the future and how well they are prepared to cater for improvements in the student's performance.

The questions in the interviews were categorised in the following ways:-

· Questions 1 and 2 sought to confirm, although not documented according to the schools supervisor's information, that there are special needs students in the mainstream schools.

· Questions 3 and 4 attempt to determine if the schools are ready to accommodate students with special needs.

All the information I received, I believe to be honest and truthful.

RELIABILITY AND VALIDITY

Bell (1993) defines reliability as:

'...the extent to which a test or procedure produces similar results under constant conditions on all occasions.' (p. 64)

In order to ensure that all respondents interpret the questionnaire questions as they were intended, care was taken in the selection of words and the syntax of the language used. Precise categories were offered where a choice was necessary so that there would be no possibility of confusion. The prepared questionnaire was piloted via e-mail, using teachers of various schools in Trinidad and Tobago. Two revisions were done and the final product was used to collect the data presented in this research.

Validity, according to Bell (1993), *'...tells us whether a question measures or describes what it is supposed to measure or describe' (p. 65).* The promise of total anonymity is one way of attempting to attain validity in responses to questions about one's practices on the job. Questions that were worded to elicit truthful and collaborative answers on a particular issue were included.

Chapter 4

Findings

PRESENTATION AND ANALYSIS OF DATA

Thirty-five questionnaires were distributed and 32 or approximately 91% were completed and returned. The other three were returned without any responses. The questionnaire was divided into two parts. The first part gathered demographic information about the teachers themselves. The second part gathered information about the education system, curriculum planning and implementation.

Figure 4.1 on page 68 shows that 25 respondents were female and four respondents were male. The other three respondents did not indicate their gender. Figure 4.1 also indicates that four teachers, all female, were eighteen to 25 years old. Eight teachers were 26 to 35 years old. They were females except for one who did not disclose his/her gender. In the largest age group, 36 to 45 years old, there were ten respondents. Eight of these were females and two were males. The 46 to 55 years age group had nine teachers. These consisted of six females, two males and one who declined to indicate his/her gender.

The over 55 age group had a lone teacher, who did not disclose his/her gender.

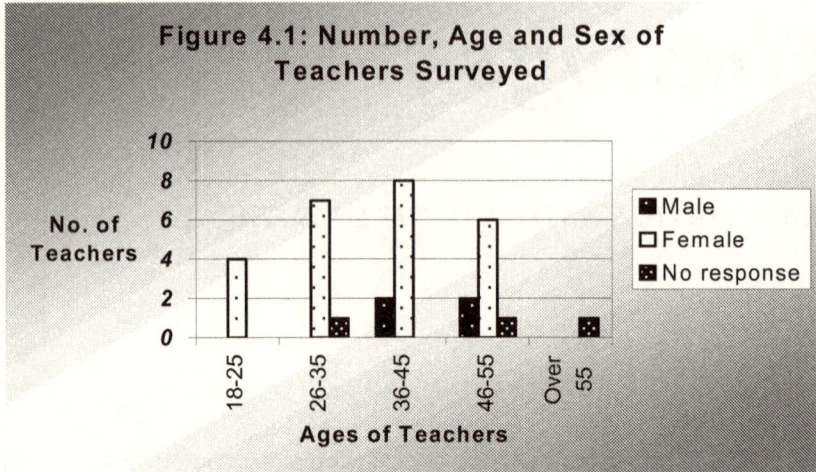

Figure 4.1: Number, Age and Sex of Teachers Surveyed

The data revealed that the majority of special schools teachers are female and the greatest numbers are those aged 36 to 45. The large drop in the number of teachers after age 55 indicated that most leave the special schools by this age.

Figure 4.2 on page 69 shows that half of the respondents in the eighteen to 25 years age group spent more than half of their short teaching careers at their present schools. On average, the group taught for four years, three of them at their present schools.

Four of the eight respondents in the 26 to 35 years age group spent at least half of their teaching careers at their present schools. On average, this group taught for nine years, five of them at the present schools.

In the 36 to 45 years age group, eight of the ten teachers spent at least half of their teaching careers at their present schools. The group, on average, taught for nineteen years, spending fifteen of them at their present schools.

Figure 4.2: Teaching Experience

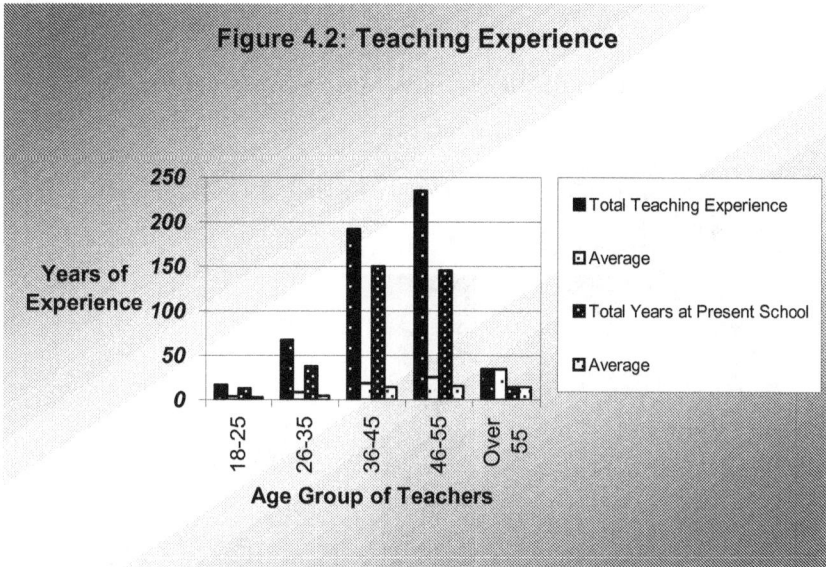

Seven of the nine teachers in the 46 to 55 years age range spent 50% or more of their careers at their present schools. This group taught for an average of 26 years and spent sixteen years at their present schools.

These responses show that there is a certain amount of commitment present in our special schools teachers. Those who believe that they are not capable would not continue to work in the special school environment for any length of time. Usually it is those who are serious and committed who endure through it all.

Figure 4.3 on page 70 demonstrates that a great majority, 28 teachers, replied yes when asked if they had formal education in Special Education. Only four stated that they did not have formal Special Education training.

Table 4.1 on page 70 divides the respondents into age groups. Of those who said they had no formal Special Education training, one of them had just one of two years experience at the present school while the other had six years teaching experience, all at the present school. They belonged to the youngest group of teachers.

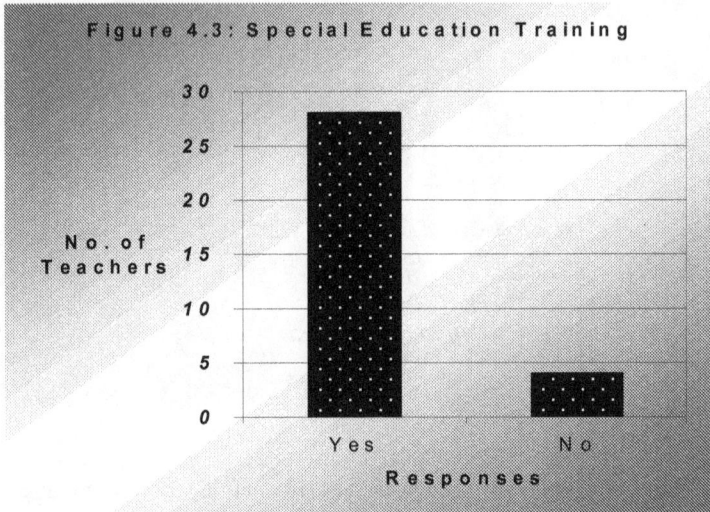

Figure 4.3: Special Education Training

Table 4.1: Have you had formal education in Special Education?

Age	Yes	No
18-25	3	2
26-35	8	0
36-45	7	2
45-55	9	0
Over 55	1	0

The other two were from the 36 to 45 years age group. One of them, with nine years' experience in teaching, had only one year's experience at his/her present school. The other had twelve years experience teaching, all at his/her present school.

Findings

Two of these teachers, however, indicated further in the questionnaire, that they attended workshops. Does this mean that these teachers do not believe that workshops are methods of educating individuals and only university courses are taken into consideration?

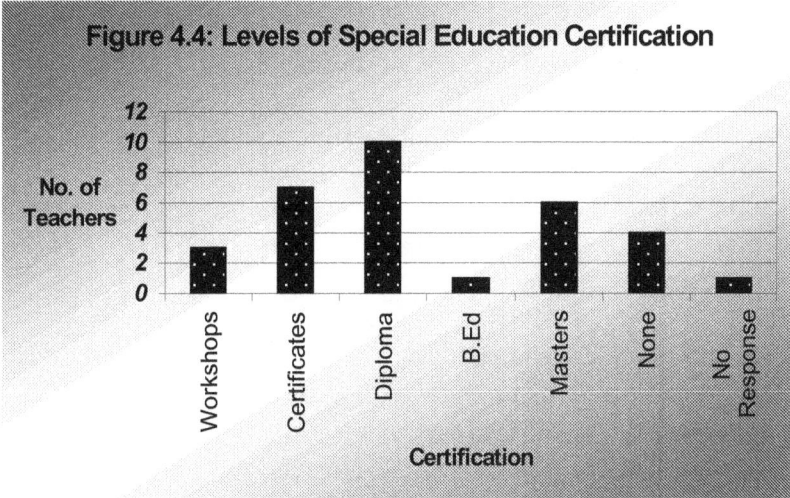

Figure 4.4: Levels of Special Education Certification

Figure 4.4 above shows three respondents attended workshops. Seven respondents earned Certificates in Special Education while ten respondents earned Diplomas in Special Education. One respondent earned a Bachelor of Education degree and six respondents earned their Masters in Special Education. Four respondents did not have any formal education in the teaching of students with special needs while one respondent chose not to submit this information.

In Trinidad and Tobago, teachers are not generally accepted into the Diploma programmes unless they undergo teacher training or earned a Bachelor's Degree. It means that seventeen of the 32 respondents were fully qualified and seven were on their way to becoming fully qualified. That would then leave 25% of special schoolteachers who will need some form of training in special education.

Question 1: **Over the last five years, what physical adaptations have been put in place at your school to cater for the special needs of children?**

Table 4.2: Adaptations Made at Schools Over the Past Five (5) Years, to Cater for the Special Needs of Children

Adaptations Identified by Teachers	# of Teachers
Adapted Desks	1
Chalkboard adaptation	1
Cooking	1
Adaptations done more than 5 years ago	1
Improvement to skills area: Computers, Beauty culture, woodwork	1
School was designed and built for special needs children	1
Technical training in Art, Computer Studies, Needlework and Cookery	1
Ramps	2
Computer rooms and computers	6
No response	6
No adaptation	11

Table 4.2 above lists adaptations, which have been put in place at special schools, to cater for the special needs of the children. Eleven teachers said that no physical adaptations were made to their schools over the past five years. Five of these teachers were at their schools for less than five years. On the other hand, one of these teachers was at his/her school for 24 years.

Of the 32 teachers who responded to this questionnaire, six did not give a response to this question. Those teachers had five to fifteen years experience at their respective schools and should be aware of any adaptations made over the last five years. If we then assume that none have been put in place, then a total of seventeen teachers had no physical adaptations put in place at their schools over the last five years.

The other fifteen teachers responded with a variety of adaptations. Six teachers reported their school(s) benefited from computer rooms and/or computers. Two teachers said their schools had ramps built. One teacher responded that his/her school was designed and built to accommodate students with disabilities while another respondent stated that physical adaptations were done on his/her school more than five years ago.

One teacher responded that desks specially adapted for special needs children were introduced to his/her school within the past five years. Another respondent said that cupboard adaptations were used. One respondent indicated that cooking was introduced, leading me to assume that a kitchen was added or was made available to the school. Another respondent stated that technical training in Art, Computer Studies Needlework and Cookery was introduced throughout the school. Yet another respondent stated that there were improvements to the skills area, computers were added, beauty culture was introduced and woodwork was revitalized.

Question 2:   Place a tick/check next to the adaptation now used at your school.

The data for this question has been divided into two tables. Tables 4.3 on page 74 and 4.4 on page 75 show the number of teachers who have the use at their school, of each adaptation mentioned in question 2. Table 4.3 below shows aids for adapting content delivery or teaching/learning aids and Table 4.4 lists the physical adaptations.

Table 4.3: Aids for Adapting Content Delivery (Teaching/Learning Aids)

AIDS	TEACHERS USING ADAPTATIONS
Computers	24
VCR's	22
Videos	20
Projector	11
Books on Tape	8
Close Captioned TV	7
Large Print Books	4
Braille	2

The three most popular adaptations fall under the category of teaching/learning aids, the most popular being computers. Twenty-four of the 32 respondents stated that they have computers available for students' use. The second most popular adaptation in the special schools surveyed is the videocassette recorder (VCR). Twenty-two teachers indicated that his/her school has at least one VCR. One of these respondents however indicated that the VCR is always locked away. This gives the impression that it is not readily available for use by teachers. Twenty of the 32 respondents indicated that videos are available for their use with students. However, there are some inconsistencies. Three of those who indicated that they have VCR's at their schools did not indicate that they have videos while one who said they had videos at the school did not indicate the presence of any

Findings

VCR at his/her school. The teacher who noted that the school's VCR is always locked away showed that there were available videos at the school.

The projector was the next popular means of transferring knowledge. Eleven of the 32 respondents stated the presence of the projector at their schools. One of these indicated that the projector was not in working condition. Four teachers have books on tape while seven teachers have closed captioned televisions. Large print books are available to four teachers and Braille is available to two teachers.

The most popular physical adaptation, as listed in Table 4.4 below, was special seating arrangements. Fourteen of the 32 respondents use special seating arrangements in the delivery of the curriculum. Wheelchairs come in second in this category with twelve teachers having these aids available at the schools.

Table 4.4: Physical Adaptations at Special Schools.

PHYSICAL ADAPTATIONS	TEACHERS INDICATING
Special seating arrangements	14
Wheelchairs	12
Adapted desks	9
Toilet rails	8
Low cupboards	7
Low door handles	5
Ramps	3
Altered playground facilities	2
Telecommunications Devices for the Deaf (TDD)	2
Low counters	1
Special lighting	1
Low resistance on doors	0

Nine teachers have adapted desks for students to work at. Eight teachers said their schools' toilets have support rails. Seven teachers indicated their schools have low cupboards and five teachers noted that their schools have low door handles. Three teachers indicated that their school(s) has/have ramps. Two teachers specified that their school(s) has/have altered playground facilities, one of these teachers indicating that the facilities need repairs. Another two said that their school(s) has/have telecommunications devices for the deaf (TDDs). One teacher did not know what a TDD was. He/She did indicate training in special education but did not specify to what level. One teacher said that his/her school has special lighting, and four said they had large print books available. Even though twelve said they have wheelchairs, just seven said their schools have low cupboards, while five said they have low door handles. Only three teachers said their schools have ramps and one teacher said there are low counters at the school. No teacher indicated low resistance on doors, a feature that would benefit students who use wheelchairs and those with muscular degenerative conditions.

This data therefore proves that the six least available adaptations at these special schools are physical adaptations. These are

     I.   Ramps: indicated by three teachers

     II.   TDD's: two teachers

     III.   Altered playground facilities: two teachers

     IV.   Special lighting: one teacher

     V.   Low counters: one teachers, and

     VI.   Low resistance on doors: no teacher.

Findings

Question 3:   Are you trained in the use of any of the above adaptations?

Figure 4.5 below identifies the number of teachers who were trained to use the adaptations mentioned in Question 2. Although all teachers should be trained to use adaptations in the classroom, the figure shows this is not so. Twenty-four of the 32 teachers surveyed had training in the use of the adaptations used at their schools. Six of the thirty-two teachers had no training and two teachers did not answer this question.

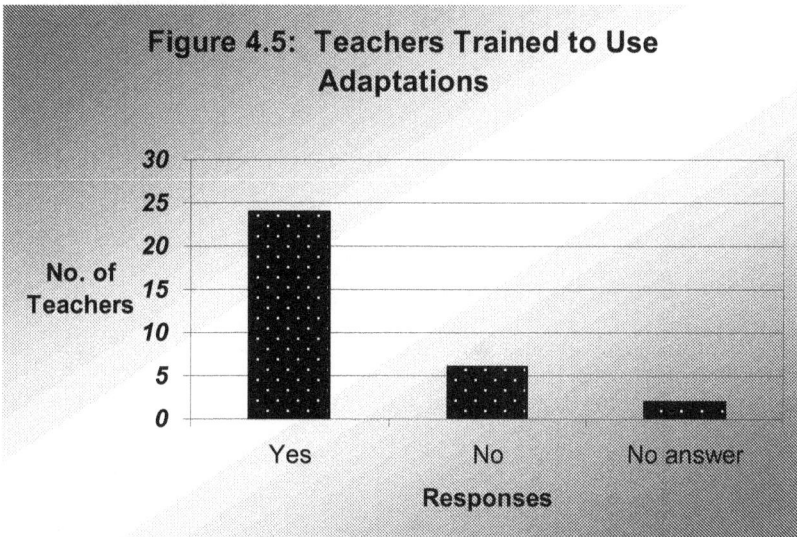

Figure 4.5: Teachers Trained to Use Adaptations

Question 4:   Do you teach using the regular school syllabus?

Figure 4.6 on page 78 reveals the number of teachers who use the regular school syllabus to teach their special needs students. Twenty-one of the 32 teachers surveyed said they teach using the regular school syllabus. Eleven teachers said they do not use the regular school syllabus. This data show that approximately one-third of special schools teachers do not follow the recommended national syllabus.

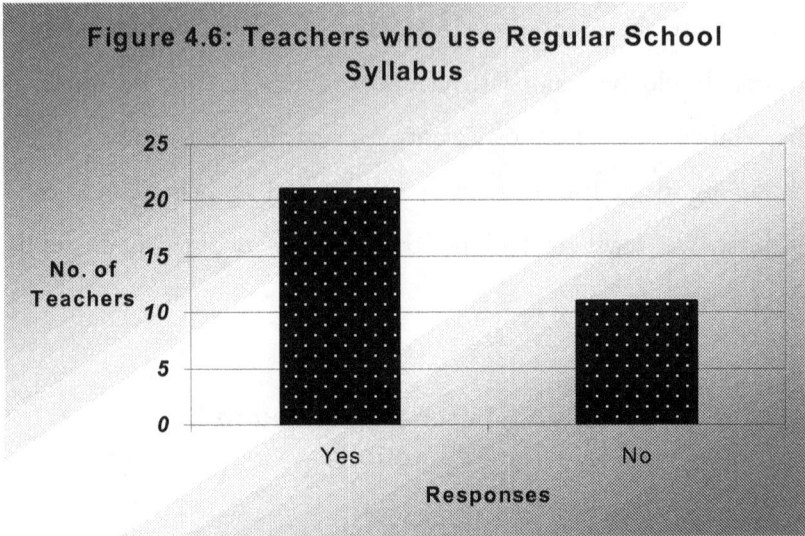

Figure 4.6: Teachers who use Regular School Syllabus

Question 5:   If yes, what adaptations do you make for the children in your class?

Of the 21 teachers who answered yes to question four, only one said that he/she teaches, using the regular syllabus, but makes no adaptations for the instruction of his/her students. The other twenty teachers named a total of 24 adaptations they use to teach students with special education needs. Table 4.5 on page 79 shows this list.

At the top of the list is task analysis. Eight teachers stated that they use task analysis as a method of instruction. Prioritising of topics according to the needs and abilities of the students is considered important, by four of the teachers. This same number of teachers allow students extended time. Re-teaching and repetition was thought

Findings

to be important enough to be mentioned by three teachers. Two teachers simply stated that they modify the primary school syllabus.

Table 4.5: Adaptations Teachers Make to the Regular Syllabus

ADAPTATIONS	NO. OF TEACHERS USING ADAPTATION
Task Analysis	8
Prioritising of Topics	4
Extended Time	4
Re-teaching/Repetition	3
Modification of Primary School Syllabus	2
Teaching Co-curricular Subjects, e.g. typing, home economics, etc.	1
Books on Tape	2
Providing a Reader	1
Photocopied Notes	1
Individual Work Cards	2
One-on-One	2
Pictures	5
Large Print	2
Charts	1
Visual Aids/Material	2
Videos	1
Projectors	1
Concrete Materials	3
Tactile Diagrams/Instruments	4
Specialised Equipment	1
Sign Language/Total Communication	2
Language Adaptation (oral, written)	1
Bliss Board	1
Other Teaching Aids	4
None	1

One teacher teaches co-curricular subjects like typing and home economics to enhance the regular curriculum. Two teachers use books on tape, and one teacher provides a peer reader to assist. Another teacher uses photocopied notes for students. Two teachers use individual work cards and the same number use one-on-one instruction.

Five teachers use pictures. Two teachers use large print books and one teacher use charts. Another two stated without elaborating, that they use visual aids. Videos and projectors are each used by one teacher.

Three teachers said they use concrete materials. Four teachers specified that they use tactile diagrams and instruments. One teacher stated that he/she uses specialised equipment.

Sign language, or total communication, is used by two teachers while oral and written language adaptation is done by one teacher.

One teacher said he/she uses bliss boards and four teachers stated that they use teaching aids. These teachers did not identify any specific aid.

Question 6: **Are there any areas of the syllabus you exclude when teaching your class? Why do you exclude them?**

Figure 4.7 on page 81 shows the number of teachers who exclude areas from the syllabus when teaching their classes.

Of the 32 teachers responding to the questionnaire, twelve of them said that they exclude areas of the syllabus when teaching their classes. One respondent specified science as the area excluded because

Findings

of a lack of resources. Another identified Science and Art as areas he/she excluded because of a lack of special manipulative equipment.

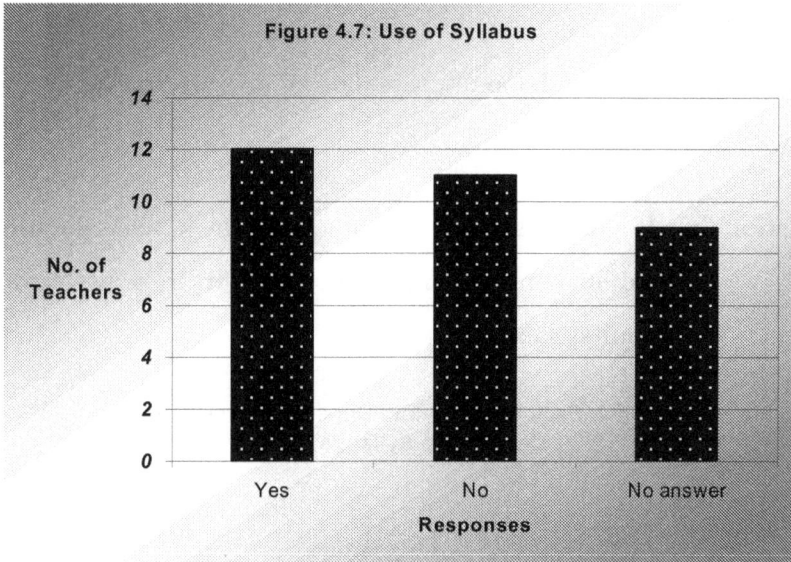

Figure 4.7: Use of Syllabus

Two teachers identified Physical Education as another excluded area. One teacher cited time constraint and a feeling that he/she is not skilled enough to teach this area. The other teacher noted that physical education is excluded throughout the school because the school does not have the necessary equipment and facilities for teaching students with physically handicapping conditions. Another respondent briefly stated a lack of facilities as the reason for omitting areas of the syllabus. One teacher noted that she excludes areas because of the students' disability and severity of this disability. He/She cited that they might not be able to hear certain musical instruments. Four teachers stated that some content is omitted because of the level of mental functioning and/or ability of the students. One teacher said that a lot of time spent on behaviour modification takes away from time spent on teaching content material. Another teacher said that he/she seldom excludes areas of the syllabus, while another said he/she excludes selected areas.

Eleven teachers said they do not exclude any area of the syllabus when teaching. Nine teachers did not give a response to this question.

Question 7: If you answered no to question 4, what factors would you take into consideration in drawing up your syllabus?

Figure 4.8: Factors Taken into Consideration when Drawing Up Syllabus.

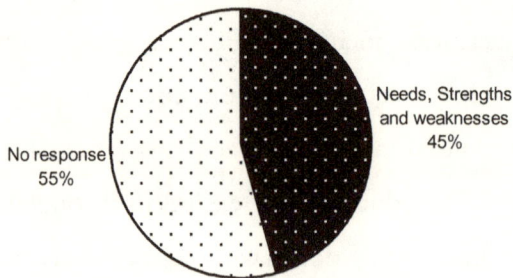

Needs, Strengths and weaknesses 45%

No response 55%

Figure 4.8 above illustrates the factors teachers take into consideration when drawing up a syllabus for their disabled charges.

Five respondents who answered no to question four take the needs, strengths and weaknesses of their students into consideration when drawing up a syllabus. One respondent identified relevance to

Findings

the needs of the child as important. Another respondent stressed the student's abilities. One thought that one should take the students needs and his/her severity of condition(s) into consideration. Another noted that the learning objectives must stay the same and we, as teachers, should try various strategies to achieve the stated objectives.

Question 8: **What are your views on mainstreaming children from your school?**

Figure 4.9: Teachers' Views on Mainstreaming Their Students

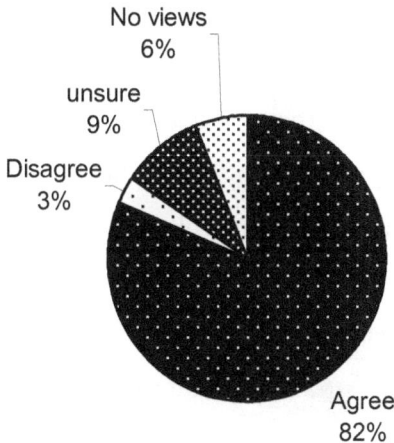

No views
6%

unsure
9%

Disagree
3%

Agree
82%

Figure 4.9 above is evidence that the great majority of teachers surveyed agreed with mainstreaming. Twenty-six of 32 teachers support mainstreaming of disabled students. They gave various reasons and identified areas that need improvement for mainstreaming to be successful. Three teachers said they were unsure of mainstreaming students from their school(s). One teacher disagreed with mainstreaming but did not give any reason. He/she had only been teaching for approximately two years, all at the same school. Two respondents had no views on mainstreaming.

Table 4:6 Teachers' Negative Views on Mainstreaming Students from their Schools

Cons of mainstreaming now	No. of teachers
Lack of personnel	7
Need for infrastructure	2
Lack of resources and organization of the system	2
School in Student's neighborhood	2
Careful consideration of Students' social/emotional state	4
Gradual mainstreaming	1
One-on-one instruction	1

Table 4.6 above lists some negative views teachers have on mainstreaming students from their special schools.

One of the teachers, who said he/she was unsure of mainstreaming, noted that it is a difficult task because of the lack of personnel. In fact, lack of school personnel was cited as a barrier to mainstreaming by seven of the 32 respondents. Two teachers identified a need for infrastructure and an equal number identified a lack of resources and organization of the system as barriers to mainstreaming.

Another two teachers noted that the student should live at home with his/her family and attend school in his/her own community. One noted that

> '...apart from their handicapping condition, added pressures and stress are placed on them and their families when they have to reside away from home to attend school' (Response to Question 8).

So we can say that

'Once there is accessibility to a school in the child's neighbourhood, the child should be allowed to attend that school' (Response to Question 8).

Ensuring accessibility to schools is the responsibility of the Ministry of Education and the Government of the country. But evidence shows that these bodies are not anxious to live up to expectations. Another teacher's response to Question 8 stated:

'Mainstreaming children from my school is a good idea in principle. However I am reluctant to view it as a positive direction because of the lethargy within the system to provide infrastructure and training for personnel in the mainstream.'

Yet another respondent noted that mainstreaming

'...is going to be extremely difficult unless personnel and resources are put into place.'

Another teacher said that there is limited mainstreaming because of a lack of personnel to service the system.

Four respondents noted that careful consideration of the students' social and emotional states should be taken when making a decision to mainstream. One respondent advocated gradual mainstreaming and another respondent noted that mainstreamed students would still need one-on-one instruction.

Table 4.7 on page 85 explains how some teachers viewed mainstreaming from a positive angle. Five teachers said that mainstreaming enables social and emotional development of the disabled child. Three teachers said that mainstreaming encourages acceptance of disabled students by their non-disabled peers. Four teachers noted that mainstreaming encourages academic challenge for both the disabled and the non-disabled student.

Five teachers agreed with mainstreaming but gave no reasons or made no comments on the process.

Table 4.7: Teachers' Positive Views on Mainstreaming Students from their Schools.

Pros of mainstreaming now	No. of teachers
Student lives with family	2
Enables social and emotional development	5
Encourages acceptance by non-disabled peers	3
Encourages academic challenges	4
Special schools can be used as resource centres	1

Question 9: In the context of your school, is it possible to mainstream children?

Figure 4.10: Possibility of Mainstreaming Children from Special Schools

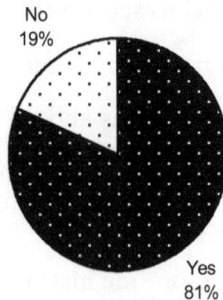

No
19%

Yes
81%

Figure 4.10 above reveals teachers' views on the possibility of mainstreaming children with special needs from their schools.

Twenty-six of the 32 teachers surveyed said that mainstreaming is possible at their schools. Six stated that mainstreaming is not at all possible at their schools.

Findings

Four teachers said that their schools are mainstreaming at present. One teacher said that his/her *'...students are already being mainstreamed via the Common Entrance Examination.'* Another teacher briefly stated that mainstreaming is currently being undertaken at his/her school. The third said that his/her school had eighteen students mainstreamed with itinerant teachers working with them at the schools they attend. One teacher said that the *'...student's social skills and communication skills are considered for mainstreaming.'*

Two teachers stated that some of their students could be mainstreamed. Other children, they said, cannot be mainstreamed because of their medical conditions and their daily needs for medical treatment. These children, they suggested, should be close to a medical facility.

One respondent noted that mainstreaming is possible at his/her school but there are not enough support systems in place. He/she also identified the need for meaningful follow-up and future-monitoring systems. Nineteen teachers said mainstreaming was possible at their schools but they did not elaborate.

Question 10:   **Could you make suggestions on how a school can improve mainstreaming?**

Question 10 asked teachers to suggest ways in which mainstreaming can be improved. Table 4.8 on page 88 lists the suggestions given by teachers. The suggestions were placed in seventeen categories involving all the major players in education. Because some teachers made more than one suggestion, the total exceeds the number of teachers surveyed.

Table 4.8: Teachers' Suggestions on Improving Mainstreaming

Suggestions to Improve Mainstreaming	No. of Teachers
Sensitise all teachers to the needs of disabled children	9
Make mainstreaming collaborative and symbiotic	8
No suggestion	7
Adapting of physcal structures	6
Appropriate support services	5
Advanced preperation of mainstream students	5
Advanced preperation of parents	4
More technogogical equipment	3
Early intervention	2
Advanced preparation of disabled students	2
Supply itinerant teachers	2
Earmark schools with trained special education teachers	2
Supply resource teachers to work with classroom teacher	2
Introduce speech teaching as early as possible to deaf	1
Discuss and plan programmes in the interest of the student	1
Supply books on time	1
Proper organisation by the Ministry of Education	1
No suggestion	7

Nine respondents recommended that mainstream teachers be sensitised to the special needs of disabled children before any mainstreaming can begin. Eight respondents suggested that mainstreaming should be a collaborative and symbiotic arrangement between and among schools. Six respondents proposed the adaptation of physical structures to allow for ease of mobility for disabled persons. One of these respondents added that the adaptations should be in place before the students are admitted. Five respondents identified appropriate support services as being necessary to improve mainstreaming. Another five suggested that mainstream students should be prepared and sensitised prior to admitting students with special needs. Four teachers added that parents should be prepared in advance of their children being joined in the mainstream by disabled peers. Three teachers said there was a need for more technological equipment in the mainstream schools. Two teachers advocated early intervention so that mainstreaming can be accomplished at an early age. Another two suggested that disabled students should be prepared in advance to enter the mainstream and cope with the demands of the schools. They further stated that the advanced preparation should take the students' emotional needs into consideration and should include such facilitating skills as typing and computer literacy. Two teachers suggested the use of itinerant teachers and another said schools with trained special education teachers should be earmarked for mainstreaming.

One teacher suggested that speech teaching should be introduced to deaf students as early as possible. Another suggested that discussions and planning of programmes should be in the interest of the student. One teacher suggested that suppliers should supply books on time and another said that we need proper organisation of the system by the Ministry of Education.

Seven teachers made no suggestions. One of them, with only two years' experience in teaching, explained that he/she had no knowledge of the process.

Question 11:   Please state any further comments you may have.

Question 11 invited any further comments that the respondents may have thought of that the researcher did not foresee. Twenty-two teachers offered none. The other ten teachers had various comments, some of which were mentioned by more than one teacher.

Two of the respondents stated that they needed more time to get information to complete the questionnaire. Complementing the questionnaire itself, a respondent stated that '...*we needed a little more time. This is a very good questionnaire'*. However, he/she did not give any response to questions 1, 2, 3, 5 and 6. The other respondent did not reply to questions 5, 6 and 10. He/she stated, *'This was too rushed; more could have been said.'*

It appears that they needed to obtain information from another source. This, I believe, would not have been accurate data because it may be duplicating information.

One teacher stated that *'More trade centres should be made available for our students'.* This may be because of the old belief that persons with special education needs do better in trade schools since they are unable to learn academic concepts and content. In contrast, another teacher saw a *'...need for special schools to rethink their focus or vision.'* This he/she saw as urgent because of *'...the many changes that are now taking place.'*

A fifth teacher commented that

'...the most difficult group to include in the common educational setting remains children with behavioural problems. No school wants to risk their "good name".'

This seems to be the reason why some principals are reported to turn away disabled children. They are afraid that their Secondary Entrance Assessment average would decrease. A sixth teacher seemed to have a solution when he/she stated that

'Resource rooms and trained resource personnel are vital to the students' successes in many ways.'

He/she then suggested: -

'Meetings with social workers, parents, principals each month after pupils have made the transition to the "normal" school.'

Findings

In agreement with the latter teacher, the seventh teacher said that

> *'...mainstreaming can be very successful with the cooperation of all stakeholders: parents, teachers, students and special teachers.'*

An eighth teacher commented that

> *'...teachers specialised in the teaching of children with special needs should be attached to mainstream schools.'*

A very expressive comment from a teacher stated:

> *'The education system of Trinidad and Tobago has wonderful rhetoric when it comes to provisions for special needs in the mainstream. Unfortunately, we have been unable to support this with the sufficient "where-with–all" to make mainstreaming a realistic or viable educational option for students with special needs.'*

The tenth teacher to offer a comment summed it all up in one sentence:

> *'The entire society needs to be incorporated in the mainstreaming effort.'*

Chapter 5

Conclusion

NEXT STEPS

THE PRESENT

In the preceding pages, I attempted to find answers to two questions. The first question asked was: -

(a) Are special schools sufficiently prepared to offer an equal chance to   students with special needs?

To answer the first research question, I found that physical adaptations were lacking most at schools.

With 19% offering no response to Question 1 and 34% indicating to this question that no adaptations were made at their schools in five years, we are left with 47%. Of the 47% who identified adaptations carried out at their schools, only 15% can be identified as physical adaptations. Therefore, 15% of the teachers surveyed indicated that some form of physical adaptation was done at their schools to cater for children with special needs. This represents a low figure when we take into consideration that only one teacher indicated that his/her school was built to accommodate all students and one other teacher stated that adaptations were made to his/her school more than five years ago.

In examining the physical adaptations now in use at special schools, it is difficult to ignore the low figures representing the number of teachers who identified the presence of these adaptations at their schools. The six (6) least available adaptations at these special schools are ramps (9%), TDD's and altered playground facilities (6% each), special lighting and low counters (3% each) and low resistance on doors (0%). These figures reveal that mobility impaired students are not well catered for at the special schools in Trinidad and Tobago.

The adaptations available to teachers and what they actually use are apparent when we compare data for Question 2 with data for Question 5. VCR's and videos are available to 22 and twenty teachers respectively. Yet only one teacher claimed to use video when teaching. Eleven teachers have projectors available to them but only one teacher claimed to use it. Of the eight teachers who claimed to have books on tape available for their use, only two actually claim to use them. Just half of the four teachers who have large print books available to them actually use them.

The second question asked: -

(b) How do teacher expectations of disabled students in special schools affect the content delivery?

To be prepared to cater for all students, schools must be staffed by well-trained and appropriately educated teachers. When we examine the levels of Special Education Certification of teachers in Special Schools, we found that 88% of special schools teachers surveyed have special education training. 75% of these teachers are

Conclusions

trained in the use of adaptations available at the schools. The majority of these teachers are committed to their students and ensured that they have the necessary training and education. The other 12% without special education training, are either young teachers just beginning in their schools, or teachers who should have had some special education training a long time ago. Two teachers 36 to 45 years old, identified by the demographic data, only attended workshops. They have been teaching for nine and twelve years. One of them has only been teaching at a special school for one year, while the other has been teaching his twelve years at the same special school. These teachers should, by now, have formal special education training. In addition, a teacher between the ages of 36 and 45 years old, working at a special school for twelve years, should be trained at least to the certificate level in special education.

There are also some 19% of teachers who are not yet trained to use adaptations at their schools. It is hoped that those who are not yet trained would avail themselves to the necessary skills needed to effectively carry out their duties as educators. Any untrained teacher in a special school can compound the problems of the students.

The majority of surveyed teachers, 66%, said they use the regular school syllabus when teaching and 63% said they do this by adapting the syllabus, to cater to the child's needs. While this is a positive idea, sufficient teachers do not use a variety of methods. For example, in identifying adaptations they make for their students, only one teacher uses charts, three teachers use concrete materials and one teacher uses specialised equipment.

The reasons given for excluding areas of the syllabus fall into two broad categories. 16% of teachers said that the severity of the students' disability makes it necessary for them to exclude area(s) of the syllabus. The other 22% identified a lack of resources and personnel as the reason for their omission of areas of the syllabus.

Dealing with special needs in the mainstream classroom would mean a change in the delivery of the curriculum. Teachers must encourage a teacher-student relationship and a teacher-parent relationship based on trust. If our parents and students know that they can trust us, we would have cooperation from both and information that would assist us in providing appropriate learning conditions and methods for individuals.

Since some children with difficulties in learning need more time, concrete examples and live experiences in order for learning to take place, we need to take our classes outside of the building and on outings more often. We should see ourselves on the field participating in sporting activities *with* our children, winning and losing and smiling.

Mainstreaming our special needs children to eventual inclusive education demands that we move away from the teacher with the middle class, authority figure and towards the friendly facilitator who will assist the students in becoming active participants in the learning process.

This may mean greater demands on our time because more planning is needed in programmes like these, and in order to be effective, we need to evaluate our programmes.

Conclusions

THE FUTURE

The issues discussed in this research paper could only be implemented if our legislators are serious about education for all. Owens (1991) notes that Parsons argues that organisations are given support from society according to the value society places on the particular function.

If we are to succeed as a people, we need to pay more attention to education and give education its rightful place as top priority. Inclusive education demands material changes in the structure of the buildings and school compounds as well as changes in the environment in society at large.

These details can be worked out by obtaining information about the necessary equipment, from the children, since they are aware of their strengths and weaknesses and know their games and their friends well.

Library facilities, rarely mentioned, pose problems to some children. Apart from the absence of ramps, installing door handles too high and not adjusting the resistance on the force used to push open the door, books are sometimes placed too high for some persons. A wheelchair user, for example, who needs a book, may find that it is on the top shelf, way out of his/her reach, requiring that he/she request someone's assistance. In addition, the seating accommodation available does not take into account the special needs of persons with disabilities.

The behaviours we display are reactions to our environment and are based on our previous experiences in the environment (Comer et. al., 1996). Human behaviour is therefore shaped by the society in which we live. Changing the individual to fit into society is therefore not the solution. The individual would have to return to the same society which shaped the unwanted behaviour; the same society, which remains unchanged. We cannot truly expect this individual to react differently towards this same environment. We must change society by educating its members to act in accordance with certain international standards, laws and ideals. The Salamanca Statement (1994), in endorsing inclusive education as a method of providing education for all in regular schools, states:

> 'Regular schools in this inclusive orientation are the most effective means of combating discriminatory attitudes, creating welcoming communities, building an inclusive society and achieving education for all;' (Quoted from C.S.I.E.; 1995, P.1).

We must note therefore, that although changes in society will be needed to implement inclusive practices in our schools, these inclusive practices themselves will be contributing to changing the society even more and as the Statement says, we would eventually build an inclusive society.

It is one thing to provide access to disabled persons but reminders to the public that these are the rights of the individual is of utmost importance in creating an inclusive society.

According to Lewis (1991), students experienced greater difficulties when transition from a special school to mainstream school took place at a later time. It would be necessary therefore to begin the transition process as early as possible. For this transition to occur, students and teachers in the mainstream schools must be prepared by lectures and workshops on rights and responsibilities and explanations of facilities and equipment for disabled persons. For disabled and non-disabled children entering school together for the first time at an early age, this introduction to each other will be less formal and will entail more of the natural process of socialisation.

So if inclusion practices begin in Early Childhood Care and Education, children would have a lot of exposure to each other in an environment, which encourages equal rights and opportunities to all. By the time the child is of primary school age, differences and difficulties would not be used to determine friendships, but similarities in personalities and in interests.

Inclusive Education would place a number of demands on our education system to satisfy the curriculum changes necessary. The White Paper recommends the use of special education teachers to cater for children with special needs. In an inclusive setting, all children with special needs would be accommodated in mainstream classes throughout the day. Therefore every teacher is responsible for all his/her students. What we need in schools are not special education teachers but inclusion specialists to assist in creating an inclusive curriculum to be used by all teachers for the benefit of all pupils.

A curriculum content which stresses academic learning and ignores vocational areas, would not be suitable to pupils with difficulties in learning, especially if the developmental aspects of the curriculum is mostly incidental. Time must be allocated to this developmental curriculum in order for some children to learn skills, which we so often take for granted. (Seba et al, 1995.)

Classroom activities should move from teachers working individually with students towards students working collaboratively on shared tasks, with the assistance and supervision of teachers. Students must move from being passive recipients to that of active participants (Seba et al, 1995.).

From the primary school, Values Education should be done, not just as a part of the Social Studies, but special emphasis should be placed on it because of the multi-ethnic and multi-cultural society in which we live (Education Policy Paper 1993 - 2003, 1993).

In the meantime, we should look at effective placement in secondary schools. Some students are lost after entering the secondary school system and subsequently leave from frustration. We must change our system to include students placed in secondary schools but not ready for secondary education.

The system should cater for remedial education in whatever area diagnosed by the Diagnostic Centre. Allowances should be made for a two or three year remedial period between primary and secondary schools, similar to the Post Primary Centre. On graduation, the student is placed either at a secondary school or a vocational school, according to the pupil's choice and performance.

The system of credits mentioned in the White Paper is a means of showing accumulated formal education experiences in the academic or vocational areas. If for some reason a student leaves the system, he/she can return at a later date and continue because he/she would have accumulated a certain number of credits.

We now need a host of new equipment and better lighting facilities to cater for the needs of all students. We also need to restructure our teacher education programme to prepare teachers to

Conclusions

cater for all children, and we need to afford adequate compensation for our teachers.

Since education provision is determined greatly by financial availability (Pilgrim, 1990; Keller, 1993; Seba et al, 1995), care must be taken in providing the type of education needed by the students in order to prevent wastage of the much-needed funds. These 'extra expenses', including recurrent expenses, should be viewed as investments in the future of our country and not as a burden to taxpayers.

REFERENCES AND BIBLIOGRAPHY

Barnes, C. and Mercer, G. (1997) 'Breaking the Mould? An introduction to doing disability research' in C. Barnes, and G. Mercer (eds) Doing Disability Research. Leeds: The Disability Press. Pp. 1 – 14.

Bartolo, P. (1995) 'The Maltese Experience' in F. Armstrong and L. Barton (eds) Comparative Perspectives on Special and Inclusive Education. Sheffield: University of Sheffield, Division of Education. Unit 8.

Bell, J. (1993) Doing Your Research Project: A Guide for First-Time Researchers in Education and Social Science – Second Edition. Buckingham: Open University Press.

Best, L. (1999) Commentary and Analysis – Pathologies born in school, Trinidad and Tobago Express Newspapers. Port of Spain: CCN Publishers. May 29, p. 13.

Brock, S., (1995) 'Accidental emancipatory action? The evolution of a project in which I learned how to work with shifting sands' In P. Potts, F. Armstrong and M. Masterton (eds) Equality and

Diversity in Education 2 – National and International Contexts. London: Routledge in association with The Open University.

Castaigne, P. (1962) The National Anthem of Trinidad and Tobago. Port of Spain: Government Printery.

Central Statistical Office (1994) Republic of Trinidad and Tobago Central Statistical Office – Statistics At A Glance 1993. Port of Spain: CSO.

Centre for Studies in Inclusive Education (1995) International Perspectives on Inclusion. Bristol: CSIE.

Chimedza, R.M. and Dzvimbo, K.P. (1995) 'Special Education in Zimbabwe' in F. Armstrong, and L. Barton (eds) Comparative Perspectives on Special and Inclusive Education. Sheffield: University of Sheffield, Division of Education. Unit 3.

Clough, P. and Lindsay (1991) Integration and the Support Services – Changing Roles in Special Education. NFER – Nelson.

Cohen, L. and Manion, L. (1994) Research Methods in Education – Fourth Edition. London: Routledge.

Coleridge, P. (1993) Disability, Liberation and Development. Oxford: Oxfam.

Comer, J.P., Haynes, N.M. and Joyner, E.T. (1996) 'The School Development Programme' in Comer et al (eds) Rallying the Whole Village – The Comer Process for Reforming Education. New York: Teachers College Press.

Fulcher, G. (1989) Disabling Policies? A Comparative Approach to Education Policy and Disability. London: Falmer Press

References and Bibliography

Government of Trinidad and Tobago (1966) <u>Laws of Trinidad and Tobago – The Education Act of 1966</u>. Port of Spain: Government Printery.

Government of Trinidad and Tobago (1985) <u>Education Plan (1985 – 1990)</u> Port of Spain: Ministry of Education.

Gowrie, G. (1993) <u>Current Issues in Sociology and Education</u>, Curepe: DCT Publishers.

Independence Exhibition Committee (1962) <u>Education 1800 – 1962 – Historical Development of Education in Trinidad and Tobago</u>. Port of Spain: Government Printing Office.

Keller, C. (1993) Lecture on 'Dominant Social Issues on Education in Trinidad and Tobago'. Valsayn Teachers' College: Unpublished.

Keller, C. et al (1993) <u>Education Policy Paper 1993 – 2003: National Task Force on Education.</u> Port of Spain: Ministry of Education.

King, S. (1982) <u>The St. Clair King Report</u>. Port of Spain: Government Printery.

Lavia, J. (1995) 'Trinidad and Tobago' in F. Armstrong and L. Barton (eds) <u>Comparative Perspectives on Special and Inclusive Education</u>. Sheffield: University of Sheffield, Division of Education.

Lewis, A. (1991) <u>Primary Special Needs and the National Curriculum</u>. London: Routledge.

London, H. A. (1994) Education Planning and Human Rights in a Developing Society – some experiences of Trinidad and Tobago, <u>Compare</u>, Vol.24, No.2, pp.127 – 137.

M.Ed. Students, Distance Learning Program, University of Sheffield (1993) <u>Written Policy – Reports, Statistics, Regulations, Laws,</u>

from Government, Schools, Regional Boards or School Councils et al. Unpublished.

Marge, M. et al (1984) <u>Report of the National Survey of Handicapped Children and Youth in Trinidad and Tobago – O.A.S./National Project in Special Education and Rehabilitation of the Handicapped.</u> Port of Spain: Government Printery.

Mason, M. (1994) 'The Breaking of Relationships' in <u>Insider Perspectives: The Voice of Disabled People.</u> Sheffield: University of Sheffield, Division of Education. Unit 5.

Ministry of Consumer Affairs and Social Services (1993) <u>Draft Policy Statement on Persons with Disabilities.</u> Port of Spain: Government Printery.

Missen, L. R. (1954) <u>Education in Trinidad and Tobago – The Report of the Working Party.</u> Trinidad, BWI: Government Printing Office.

O'Leary, M. (1997) Education and training needs and the EU response – The case of Somalia 1991 – 1997, <u>The Courier: Africa – Caribbean – Pacific – European Community.</u> No 162, March – April, Brussels: EU. Pp. 64 – 66.

Oliver, M. (1994) 'Politics and Language: Understanding the Disability Discourse' in L. Barton (ed) <u>Insider Perspectives: The Voice of Disabled People.</u> Sheffield: University of Sheffield, Division of Education. Unit 3.

Oliver, M. (1997) 'Emancipatory Research – Realistic Goal or Impossible Dream?' in C. Barnes and G. Mercer (eds) <u>Doing Disability Research.</u> Leeds: The Disability Press. Pp. 15 – 31.

References and Bibliography

Paranjpe, S. (1994) A community-based model of integration for primary education in India – a focus on SLD, <u>European Journal of Special Needs Education</u>. Vol. 9, No. 2. pp. 152 – 167.

Pilgrim, E. (1990) <u>National Consultation on Special Education</u>. Port of Spain: Government Printery.

Rioux, M.H., Crawford, C., Ticoll, M., and Bach, M. (1997) 'Uncovering the Shape of Violence – A Research Methodology Rooted in the Experience of People With Disabilities' in C. Barnes and G. Mercer (eds) <u>Doing Disability Research</u>. Leeds: The Disability Press. Pp. 190 – 206

Seba et al (1995) <u>Redefining the Whole Curriculum for Pupils with Learning Disabilities</u>. London: David Fulton.

UNESCO (1994) <u>The Salamanca Statement and Framework for Action on Special Needs Education</u>. Paris: UNESCO.

United Nations General Assembly (1948) <u>Universal Declaration of Human Rights</u>. New York: UNDP.

United Nations General Assembly (1959) <u>Declaration on the Rights of the Child</u>. New York: UNDP

United Nations General Assembly (1989) <u>Convention on the Rights of the Child</u>. New York: UNDP

United Nations General Assembly (1993) <u>United Nations Standard Rules on the Equalisation of Opportunities for Persons with Disabilities</u>. New York: UNDP

Vasey, S (1994) 'The Experience of Disability' in L. Barton (ed) <u>Insider Perspectives</u>. Sheffield: University of Sheffield, Division of Education. Unit 4.

Williams, E. E. (1970) <u>From Columbus to Castro – The History of the Caribbean, 1492 – 1969</u>. London: Andre Deutsch.

Williams, E. E. (1962) <u>History of the People of Trinidad and Tobago</u>. Port of Spain: PNM Publishing.

List of Appendices

December 1, 2000

Dear Educators,

As part of my studies towards the M.Ed. in Special and Inclusive Education with the University of Sheffield, I am required to submit a dissertation based on a research project. Can you please assist me by completing the following questionnaire?

I assure you that the names of individuals and schools will NOT be included or implied anywhere in the report. A copy of the report will be available in the TTUTA library.

Sincerely,

....

Rodney A. Libert

Comprehensive Special Educator

Connecticut, USA

TEACHER QUESTIONNAIRE

Circle the appropriate response.

➤ Male   Female

➤ Age Group   18 – 25   26 – 35   36 – 45

                        46 – 54   Over 55

➤ Have you had formal education in Special Education?

       Yes   No

➤ What level of special education certification have you completed?

       Workshop   Certificate   Diploma   Masters

➤ Give answer to the nearest year completed

       Years of experience   _____

       Years at present school   _____

1. Over the last five (5) years, what physical adaptations have been put in place at your school to cater for the special needs of children?

_____

_____

_____

_____

2. Place a tick next to the adaptation(s) now used at your school

    *Projector   *Braille   *special lighting

    *large print books   *books on tape   *ramps

    *low cupboards   *low counters   *VCRs

    *low door handles   *videos   *TDDs

    *low resistance on doors   *toilet rails   *adapted desks

    *altered playground facilities   *Close Captioned TV's

         *wheelchairs

    *special seating arrangements   *computers for students' use

3. Are you trained in the use any of the above adaptations?

           Yes   No

4. Do you teach your students using the regular school syllabus?

           Yes   No

5. If yes, what adaptations do you make for the instruction of the children in your class?

    _____

    _____

    _____

6. Are there areas of the syllabus you exclude when teaching your class? Why do you exclude them?

_____

_____

_____

7. If you answered no to question 4, what factors were taken into consideration in drawing up your syllabus?

_____

_____

_____

8. What are your views on mainstreaming children from your school?

_____

_____

_____

9. In the context of your school, is it possible to mainstream children?

_____

_____

_____

10. Could you make suggestions on how a school can improve mainstreaming?

_____

_____

_____

11. Please state any further comments you may have.

_____

_____

_____

_____

_____

_____

Thank you for your time and your patience.

The Chief Education Officer,
Ministry of Education,
Alexandra Street,
St Clair,
Port of Spain.

Sir,

I, Rodney Andre Libert, hereby seek your permission to conduct research on the delivery of Special Education in selected schools in Trinidad and Tobago.

This is necessary as part-fulfilment of the Masters in Education Degree in Special and Inclusive Education from the University of Sheffield. I am a registered part-time student of the Distant Learning Programme, Student No. 959017702.

I look forward to an early reply so that I would complete my dissertation in time for submission by the July 30, 1998 deadline.

I remain,

Yours respectfully,

....

Rodney Andre Libert, Teacher 1

Cascade School for the Deaf.

The Chief Education Officer,
Ministry of Education,
Alexandra Street,
St. Clair,
Port of Spain.

Sir,

This is a follow-up to an application I made in August 1997, seeking permission to conduct research in the delivery of Special Education in schools in Trinidad and Tobago. My previous application was misplaced and I have since migrated to the United States, hence the delay in the follow-up.

This is necessary as part-fulfilment of the Masters in Education Degree in Special and Inclusive Education from the University of Sheffield. I am a registered part-time student of the Distant Learning Programme, Student No. 959017702.

I look forward to an early reply.

Yours sincerely,

....

Rodney Andre Libert, T.Dip.(VTC), Dip.Sp.Ed.(Shef)

Connecticut, USA

Does It Infringe on the Human Rights of Disabled Students?

www.ingramcontent.com/pod-product-compliance
Lightning Source LLC
Chambersburg PA
CBHW031212270326
41931CB00006B/531